# Iceland Travel Guide

The Comprehensive Guide to Embark on a Journey Through Breathtaking Landscapes, Cultural Marvels, and Epic Adventures in the Land of Glaciers and Volcanoes

**Elias Goddson**

# Table of Contents

# Introduction

**Welcome to Iceland: An Unforgettable Adventure in the Land of Natural Wonders**

A location where fire and ice dance together, where mystical landscapes captivate the soul, and where ancient sagas resound through the winds come to mind. Picture yourself standing on the edge of a roaring waterfall, feeling the mist on your face as the sheer strength of nature takes your breath away. Imagine yourself amidst a fantastical setting where you feel like you've entered a world of magic and myth. Welcome to Iceland, a place of spectacular panoramas and unmatched beauty. This tiny island nation is a world of treasures just waiting to be discovered, nestled in the North Atlantic Ocean.

As soon as your feet touch Icelandic soil, you will be submerged in the untamed environment that characterizes this amazing location. Every area of Iceland displays the magnificence and tenacity of nature, from the roaring torrents of waterfalls to the serene tranquillity of geothermal hot springs. Get ready to be mesmerized by this region of opposites, where glaciers cohabit with volcanoes and thriving towns coexist with unspoiled, desolate landscapes.

If you're reading this, you likely long for an experience that will forever change you. You yearn for an adventure that goes beyond the usual, for a chance to flee the every day and slam into a world where every minute is spectacular. But perhaps the sheer number of options has you feeling disoriented or unsure of where to begin. It's not just you.

It cannot be easy to plan a trip to Iceland. There are numerous considerations and details to consider, from choosing which natural wonders to visit to determining the optimum time to visit. It's simple to get lost in a sea of knowledge and want a reliable friend to lead you through this magical region.

This book fills that need. The Iceland Travel Guide is your compass and road map for discovering this amazing island's mysteries. Discover hidden jewels and must-see places, as well as great insights and useful recommendations to make your travel effortless and unforgettable by immersing yourself in the pages ahead.

The following chapters will teach you about some of Iceland's most famous sites, including the breathtaking Blue Lagoon and the majestic Golden Circle. You'll dig into the mystique of Iceland's fabled folklore, where you'll come across elves, trolls, and sagas that have influenced the country's culture for generations. The finest times to see the hypnotic Northern Lights dance across the Arctic sky will be revealed, and you'll learn insider tricks for getting that picture-perfect Instagram snap.

I bring my firsthand knowledge and intense passion for all things Icelandic as your trustworthy guide to this book. I am familiar with the excitement and difficulties of an Icelandic trip, having explored the stunning landscapes, trekked the volcanic terrains, and soaked in the geothermal hot springs. I have invested countless hours in research, location scouting, and building relationships with local specialists to ensure this book is thorough, trustworthy, and filled with the most recent information.

So, if you're prepared to travel somewhere that will spark your imagination, awaken your senses, and leave you with lifelong memories, look no further. The best book for you is The Iceland Travel Guide. We'll travel through glaciers, negotiate harrowing fjords, and take in the ethereal grandeur of the Midnight Sun together. Get ready to explore a place where amazement has no bounds and nature rules supreme. Your Icelandic journey is waiting!

## Why Visit Iceland: Irresistible Reasons to Choose the Island as Your Travel Destination

The Nordic Island nation of Iceland is appropriately known as the "Land of Fire and Ice." The contrast of scorching lava and ice creates a spectacular landscape that catches the heart of every traveler. The area is teeming with active volcanoes and enormous glaciers. You discover an island rich in natural beauty and cultural diversity as you explore Iceland's wonders.

### Iceland: A Traveler's Paradise

Iceland hailed as a traveler's paradise, offers a fusion of enthralling wilderness and energetic city life. The capital, Reykjavik, is teeming with hip restaurants, museums, and galleries, while the surrounding countryside is home to tumbling waterfalls, hot springs, and geysers. Iceland is an alluring destination because of this appealing combination, which guarantees it can satisfy many travelers' interests.

### Untouched Wilderness and Wide-Open Spaces

Iceland's unspoiled landscape offers a haven for people looking for peace. The nation offers countless options for exploration, from the Highlands' pristine, natural splendor to the vast, arid deserts created by volcanic eruptions. You'll discover peace as you go through the wide open spaces, surrounded by the beauty of nature.

## The Splendor of Icelandic Landscapes

Icelandic landscapes are breathtakingly beautiful. Geysers, hot springs, and harsh terrain give Iceland its distinctive geophysical character, or "Icelandia," as academics refer to the submerged continent beneath the island. You will be fascinated by the country's natural magnificence, whether hiking through green valleys or climbing snow-capped mountains.

## Beauty Beyond the Crowds: Why Iceland is Europe's Least-Populated Gem

Iceland, the least populous nation in Europe, makes for an excellent getaway from busy tourist areas. Iceland is an undiscovered gem with a population density of just three persons per square kilometer. Without the clamor of busy tourists, explore vast fjords, stroll on black sand beaches, or take in the awe-inspiring glaciers.

## An Encounter with Iceland's People

Embrace the Ultra-friendly Locals

The friendliness and generosity of Icelanders are well known. Locals are always willing to offer fascinating stories from Icelandic folklore, show you undiscovered natural attractions, or suggest the best local cuisine. This genuine engagement will undoubtedly improve your Icelandic vacation.

## The Peaceful Nation: The Icelandic Way of Life

Iceland, which routinely scores highly on the Global Calm Index, is a refuge of peace. Visitors may find the peaceful way of life in the nation to be a welcome change due to the low crime rate, high levels of social trust, and general lack of aggressive behavior among the populace.

## Fresh Air and Clean Environment

The Purity of the Icelandic Atmosphere

Thanks to its beautiful surroundings, Iceland has some of the cleanest air on the planet. Low population density and the absence of big industry lead to little pollution, leaving the air clean and revitalizing.

Connect with Nature in the Cleanest Air on Earth

Exploring Iceland's outdoor wonders while inhaling the country's clean air is an experience. The crisp Icelandic air enhances the enjoyment of these activities, whether hiking on historic glaciers or seeing the Northern Lights.

## Equality and Language

Leading the World: Gender Equality in Iceland

Due to its strict rules ensuring equal pay and opportunities, Iceland is a global leader in gender equality. Another example of Iceland's progressive mentality is the country's tangible commitment to gender equality in day-to-day affairs.

English is widely spoken throughout the nation, even though Icelandic, a North Germanic language, continues to be the official language. Tourists may easily travel about Iceland, and linguists can explore the nuances of the Icelandic language.

## The Natural Phenomenon: The Midnight Sun

Exploring the Midnight Sun Phenomenon

Thanks to the Midnight Sun, the land is bathed in continuous daylight during the summer months, allowing you extra time to explore. The bizarre lighting creates amazing photo opportunities and gives the scenery a fantastic quality.

## The Northern Lights

The Northern Lights are an amazing sight that may be seen in Iceland. The sight of auroras swirling their colors in the pitch-black Arctic sky is unforgettable.

## Hunting the Northern Lights: An Unforgettable Experience

The pursuit of the elusive Northern Lights is a once-in-a-lifetime adventure. The thrill of seeing one of nature's most magical displays brings the suspense and excitement of the hunt to a satisfying conclusion.

## Iceland's Geothermal Baths

Geothermal pools in Iceland provide a stimulating experience. Relaxation and healing are mixed as you soak in naturally heated pools while immersed in steam and enjoying the lovely scenery.

## The Blue Lagoon and Beyond Discovering Iceland's Natural Pools

The most well-known of Iceland's natural geothermal pools is the Blue Lagoon, although the country is peppered with many more. These undiscovered treasures provide tranquil locations for a relaxing dip away from the typical tourist routes.

### Spectacular Wildlife: Whales and Puffins

For lovers of wildlife, whale watching in Iceland is a must-do activity. Discover a variety of species in the nearby oceans, from fun humpback whales to majestic blue whales.

### Puffins: Encounter with the Iconic Birds of Iceland

Puffins are fascinating to see because of their recognizable multicolored beaks. During the summer, thousands of these endearing birds build nests on the seaside cliffs, providing an appealing sight for both birdwatchers and photographers.

### The Diverse Landscape of Iceland

Discover Iceland's Diverse Landscape, from Ice to Green

Iceland's views change dramatically from snow-capped glaciers to lush valleys, black sand beaches, to imposing volcanoes. This variety of natural marvels shows Iceland's astonishing geographic diversity.

Magnificent Volcanoes and Magnificent Waterfalls

Volcanoes are a significant component of Iceland's landscape. An erupting volcano's molten lava flow is a powerful reminder of nature's unbridled power. In addition to famous flowing waterfalls like Gullfoss, the nation has other views that will awaken you by nature's artistic prowess.

### The Mountain Hiking Adventure

Colorful Peaks: Hiking in Landmannalauger

A hiker's dream, Landmannalauger is noted for its multicolored rhyolite mountains and geothermal pools. Every hike is a wonderful experience, thanks to the trails that crisscross the vivid terrain and give picturesque views at every turn.

Take a Risk and Investigate Iceland's Distinctive Mountain Ranges

Outdoor enthusiasts will find special challenges in Iceland's mountain ranges. Every trail offers you wonderful solitude and breathtaking views, whether it's the troll-like peaks of the Hornstrandir Nature Reserve or the rough terrain of the Westfjords.

## The Icelandic Cuisine

Taste the Unique Icelandic Cuisine

Icelandic food is a journey through the nation's traditions and creativity. The flavors of Iceland are likely to tempt your taste buds, from local lamb to exquisite skyr, fresh seafood to pickled shark.

Iceland's Traditional Foods and Where to Find Them

Learn about the diversity of traditional Icelandic cuisine. Savor the creamy texture of Plokkfiskur, a cup of substantial Lamb soup, or the notorious Hakarl. Whatever you decide, a culinary journey is guaranteed with Icelandic cuisine.

Put Iceland on your travel wish list for its diversified landscapes, friendly population, rare natural phenomena, and rich culinary tradition, to name just a few reasons. Iceland travel offers many opportunities for adventure, leisure, and cultural immersion. This kingdom of fire and ice welcomes you to discover its numerous treasures and depart with lifelong memories.

## Basic Information: Geography, Climate, Culture, and Practical Tips to Know

Iceland, an island nation in the North Atlantic Ocean, offers a vibrant symphony of contrasts in its climate, topography, and culture. This chapter will envelop you in the essence of this fascinating nation by providing a detailed analysis of its physical geography, climatic quirks, rich cultural heritage, and useful travel advice.

### Geography

Iceland, located on the geological fault line between North America and Europe, is a region of spectacular geological activity. Iceland, which has an area larger than all of Europe's glaciers and is home to Vatna Glacier (Vatnajökull), Europe's biggest glacier, is a picture of untamed beauty.

It's interesting to note that roughly 10% of the nation is covered in a layer of glacier ice and cooled lava. A raised plateau characterizes the landscape, dotted with mountain peaks, ice fields, and fjords—deep inlets sculpted by glaciers—creating an impressive shoreline. The size of Iceland is comparable to that of the state of Kentucky, and it is situated northwest of the UK.

### Climate

Despite its name and closeness to the Arctic Circle, Iceland enjoys a temperate climate because of the Gulf Stream. Summers are cool, and winters are pleasant due to the marine climate. Average summertime temperatures range from 10 to 13°C (50 to 55°F), with longer daytime hours. With an average temperature of 0°C (32°F), winters are considered mild.

But Iceland's weather has a reputation for being erratic, changing in hours and occasionally accommodating a wide range of meteorological events in a single day. Strong winds and numerous storms can be unleashed in the winter.

## Culture

The population of Iceland, the oldest democracy in the world, is overwhelmingly of Scandinavian heritage. Preserving traditions, rituals, and language is a defining aspect of Icelandic culture. Some residents still hold onto the fabled creatures like elves and trolls, which have roots in the land's Celtic and Norse origins.

Despite its modernity, the inhabitants of Iceland have a romanticized image of it as a pastoral place where stories from their Norse past are intermingled with modern life. All Icelanders are entitled to a free education that lasts through college and includes instruction in both Danish and English. Sports, including handball, soccer, swimming, and horseback riding, are popular with kids.

## Practical Tips to Know

Due to the unpredictability of the weather, packing sensibly is required for a trip to Iceland. It is essential to dress appropriately, with layers for different weather situations. Pay attention to local advisories and weather forecasts, especially in the winter.

Since most Icelanders speak English well, communication is usually simple for visitors. Respectful conversation and behavior are crucial because local customs and traditions are highly valued. The nation is renowned for having a strong environmental conscience. Thus, you should respect nature while staying on the approved pathways.

Don't miss the distinctive local food, which offers a blend of traditional and cutting-edge delicacies, for an authentic Icelandic experience. Your palate is in for a treat, with everything from fermented shark to the well-known Icelandic hot dog.

Iceland guarantees a breath-taking encounter with nature, whether the volcanoes, the geysers, the Northern Lights, or the Midnight Sun enchant you. A visit to this country of fire and ice is an astonishing immersion into the heart of the North Atlantic; it offers a rare combination of mystical vistas and dynamic culture.

As you embark on your Icelandic adventure, you must be prepared and equipped with the knowledge to enhance your experience. The following chapters will provide practical tips and essential information to ensure a smooth and enjoyable journey.

From understanding Iceland's unique geography and climate to navigating the intricacies of local customs and etiquette, we aim to empower you with the tools to make the most of your time in this captivating country. We will guide you through the intricacies of planning your trip, from choosing the best time to visit to creating an itinerary that suits your interests. We will also offer insights into transportation options, accommodation choices, and budget management, so you can make informed decisions that align with your travel preferences.

We pledge to give you a genuine and meaningful vacation experience while preserving your security and well-being. We will advise you on safe travel procedures and urge you not to harm Iceland's delicate ecosystems or cultural heritage.

As you turn the pages of this guide, be prepared to embark on a journey that will awaken your senses, broaden your horizons, and leave an indelible mark on your soul. Iceland offers a unique experience, from its scenery's untamed splendor to its people's welcoming embrace.

Let the excitement grow as we explore the chapters in store for you. Explore the famed Golden Circle and Reykjavik, Iceland's dynamic capital city, to learn more about its treasures. Explore the ethereal worlds of glaciers and volcanoes while strolling along the South Coast. Take in the Highlands' peace and wildness and the North's tranquillity. Enjoy the delights of Icelandic cuisine while engaging with the distinctive culture.

Welcome to Iceland, where there is excitement around every corner. Prepare yourself to make lifelong memories.

# Chapter 1: Trip Preparation

### Planning Your Trip: Timelines, Itineraries, and Logistics

A thrilling excursion that offers numerous experiences, fascinating landscapes, and life-long memories is exploring the Land of Fire and Ice. This detailed guide will assist you in planning your ideal Icelandic vacation.

### Choosing the Best Season for Your Adventure in Iceland

Iceland is unquestionably a refuge for travelers, brimming with beautiful scenery and one-of-a-kind experiences. Although the country's beauty is constant throughout the year, each season has its distinctive appeal and creates various experiences that turn each trip into a new adventure. Depending on the experiences you want to enjoy, you can choose the best time to visit this Nordic beauty. So let's travel around the Icelandic calendar and see what surprises each season has for you.

**Summer (June to August): The Midnight Sun and Endless Exploration**

Icelandic summers are a heavenly display that goes above and beyond the norm. This time of year brings about the Midnight Sun, a celestial phenomenon caused by the tilt of the Earth's axis. This fascinating phenomenon casts a permanent golden glow over the Icelandic landscapes, resulting in an ethereal atmosphere that lasts late into the night.

Exploring Iceland in the summer offers countless opportunities for discovery. Imagine walking along lush pathways as the sun dips below the horizon, following a flashlight at midnight, or exploring isolated fjords' hidden caverns in the soft light of day. The landscape is dotted with waterfalls just waiting to be discovered in all their majesty.

For those who find comfort in nature's embrace, the season is transformed into a paradise. Outdoor activities such as hiking, bird viewing, and camping in breathtaking settings await, allowing you to fully immerse yourself in the vibrant natural splendor that Iceland perpetually delivers.

**Winter (December to February): Chasing the Northern Lights and Winter Wonders**

Iceland becomes a country of winter delights as the summer sun gives way to winter's cold touch. The elusive display of the Northern Lights defines this season's classic beauty. These ethereal dancers brighten the winter nights, their dazzling colors dancing across the sky in a show that astounds onlookers.

The scenery changes into a snow-covered canvas with ice-covered waterfalls and mountains in stark contrast. Such stunning views are best enjoyed while participating in various winter activities that only enhance the pleasure. Imagine riding a snowmobile through immense glaciers covered in snow or soaking in geothermal hot springs surrounded by freezing scenery. Adventurers can set out on a thrilling trek into the complex ice caves, which offer an experience from a winter fairy tale.

**Spring (March to May) and Autumn (September to November): Off-Peak Adventures and Changing Landscapes**

Iceland finds itself in the throes of two transitional seasons, spring and autumn, each bringing a distinct blend of sensations as summer departs and winter looms or vice versa. The landscapes are painted with vivid hues of blooming wildflowers or the rich hues of fall leaves during these shoulder seasons, which are times of change.

With the return of migratory birds and the sight of vivid plants poking through the thawing earth, spring ushers in a new chapter. On the other side, autumn is a splendid exhibition of nature getting ready for the upcoming cold season, painting the landscapes with a riot of warm hues that gorgeously reflect in the lakes' crystal clear waters.

Those wishing to avoid the summer crowds can take advantage of these off-peak times for a more relaxing and reasonably priced experience. Accommodations are more easily accessible, and major sites can be explored without crowds. It allows one to interact closely with nature and see how landscapes change, transforming each moment into a treasured memory.

Each season in Iceland offers a distinct, alluring experience that can be tailored to various tastes and activities. There is never a bad season to visit Iceland, whether it's the eternal summer sunshine, the celestial display of the winter, or the changing beauty of spring and autumn. When you decide to travel to this magical nation will only be determined by the experiences and memories you long to have.

## Decide How Long to Stay

The duration of your trip will depend on your interests and the size of the nation you decide to visit. You could allot a week or two to discover Reykjavik's charms and those of its surroundings. However, if you want to travel the entire Ring Road, you must prepare to commit at least a fortnight to this lengthy expedition.

## Itineraries

Having a detailed plan when traveling is crucial, especially on a trip as diverse and expansive as one to Iceland. It provides a timetable of the must-see places, the hidden jewels, and the unexpected, saving you time and stress and acting as a roadmap for your vacation. Travelers can avoid missing out on this exciting country's experiences by planning their trip and staying organized. It's a customized tour of Iceland that considers your preferences regarding pace, price, and interests.

## A Five-Day Adventure into Iceland's Richness

**Day 1:** Start at the nation's capital, Reykjavik, and acquaint yourself with its thriving culture. Start with the city's historic church, Hallgrmskirkja, which offers sweeping vistas. Visit the Harpa Concert Hall next, a magnificent building that serves as a venue for diverse concerts. Take a culinary journey to cap off your day in Reykjavik's world-famous food district.

**Day 2:** Leave the city behind and travel the Golden Circle, a well-known circuit that includes some of Iceland's most breathtaking vistas. Visit the impressive Gullfoss waterfall, Geysir Geothermal Area, and Ingvellir National Park.

**Day 3:** Go for a drive along the South Coast, which features stunning black-sand beaches like Reynisfjara. Visit Seljalandsfoss and Skógafoss waterfalls, then spend the evening at the farthest-southern hamlet of Vk.

**Day 4:** Visit Skaftafell in Vatnajökull National Park, which boasts hiking routes and glaciers. Discover the stunning Diamond Beach and Jökulsárlón glacier lagoon.

**Day 5:** Before returning to Reykjavik, stop by the Blue Lagoon, a geothermal spa famed for its therapeutic benefits. Return to the city and spend your final evening enjoying the nightlife after a therapeutic soak.

**The Perfect Weekend Getaway in Iceland**

**Day 1:** Arrive in Reykjavik and immediately depart for the Golden Circle. A brief yet insightful look into Iceland's geological marvels, history, and natural beauty is provided by this route. The Secret Lagoon in Flir is a lesser-known hot spring that is excellent for relaxing. Don't miss it.

**Day 2:** Driving to the South Coast, visit the captivating Reynisfjara black sand beach and the breathtaking Solheimajokull glacier. To round off your weekend experience, head back to Reykjavik for a stroll around the Old Harbor in the evening and a delicious Icelandic supper.

**The Ultimate Icelandic Couples Retreat**

**Day 1:** Once in Reykjavik, stroll around the charming, picture-perfect streets, stopping at neighborhood cafes and stores. A lovely sunset may be seen in the Sun Voyager sculpture.

**Day 2:** Together, explore the Golden Circle while taking in the beauty and quiet of Ingvellir National Park. Then have dinner by candlelight when you get back to Reykjavik.

**Day 3:** Discover the waterfalls and black sand beaches on the South Coast. Relax in the evening at one of Vk's cozy eateries.

**Day 4:** Take an exciting glacier hike at Skaftafell, deepening your relationship. Watch the Northern Lights together at night for a once-in-a-lifetime experience.

**Day 5:** Treat yourselves to a relaxing trip to the Blue Lagoon before you depart, and let the healing waters refresh you. Enjoy a spa treatment as a pair while sipping sparkling wine as you toast your Icelandic journey.

These itineraries provide several ways to explore Iceland's enchanted landscape. Every tourist can find the perfect itinerary, whether they want a five-day immersive trip, a quick weekend break, or a private getaway for two. While making sure you discover Iceland's breathtaking sights and undiscovered jewels, a well-planned itinerary enables you to experience the spontaneity of travel. Accept the challenge; being aware of your schedule will give you a wonderful trip across Iceland.

**A Family-Friendly Icelandic Adventure**

**Day 1:** Visit the Reykjavik Zoo and the family-friendly Whales of Iceland Exhibition to kick off your trip to Reykjavik. Bring a picnic to the tranquil Grasagardur Botanical Garden in the city.

**Day 2:** Start your journey around the Golden Circle, stopping at the Geysir Geothermal Area. Children will be ecstatic to witness the Strokkur geyser explode.

**Day 3:** Visit the Skógafoss waterfall on the South Coast, where kids can play freely and enjoy the legends of hidden wealth there.

**Day 4:** Visit the Njardvk Viking World Museum before continuing to the Blue Lagoon. Children will enjoy splashing around in the warm pool just as much as adults enjoy the soothing waters.

**Day 5:** Visit the interactive Perlan Museum in Reykjavik to complete your tour of Iceland's natural treasures. After that, stroll through Laugardalur Park, which features a zoo, a botanical garden, and entertaining family activities.

**A Solo Traveler's Icelandic Itinerary**

**Day 1:** Start your adventure by walking around Reykjavik's streets and visiting the National Museum of Iceland to learn about the nation's history. Investigate Reykjavik's live music scene in the evening.

**Day 2:** Explore the Golden Circle, stopping at each location to fully absorb it. Take a side trip to the stunningly beautiful volcanic crater known as Keri Crater Lake.

**Day 3:** Drive along the South Coast and enjoy the seclusion at Reynisfjara's black sand beach. Simply savor the beauty all around you for a moment.

**Day 4:** A solitary journey would not be complete without a challenging hike. For breathtaking vistas, visit the Skaftafell wilderness area in Vatnajökull National Park.

**Day 5:** Spend your final day relaxing at the Blue Lagoon, or if you're up for a little more adventure, depart from Reykjavik's Old Harbor on a whale-watching excursion. Finally, toast your productive solo trip with a farewell meal at one of the best restaurants in the area.

**A Weekend Break for Adventure Seekers**

**Day 1:** Take on the Golden Circle with a twist by combining the sightseeing with a snowmobile tour on the Langjökull glacier to kick off your brief but action-packed journey.

**Day 2:** As you go to the South Coast, stop at Seljalandsfoss and Skógafoss for some exhilarating ice climbing. Later, challenge yourself with a hike on Sólheimajökull's glacier.

These itineraries can accommodate a variety of travel preferences, whether traveling with a significant other, your family, or on your own through Iceland. They provide a variety of well-known sights and undiscovered treasures, guaranteeing that every day in Iceland is filled with brand-new adventures. A thorough plan will save you time and effort and guarantee you get the most out of your vacation. Remember that these itineraries are just a starting point; feel free to modify them to fit your particular preferences and travel style to make your Icelandic adventure special. Travel safely!

# Entry Requirements: Passport, Visa, and Other Important Information

Iceland has always been a well-liked destination for tourists looking to experience its distinctive culture and gorgeous surroundings since it is a magnificent Nordic island country. As with any other country, entering this requires the appropriate papers, and depending on the traveler's nationality, there are frequently additional requirements.

## Travel under the Schengen Agreement

Iceland's participation in the Schengen Agreement is a significant factor that influences the country's admission criteria. This pact covers 26 nations throughout Europe and does away with passport checks and visa requirements at shared borders. This agreement provides visa-free stays of up to 90 days in Iceland for tourism or business purposes for citizens of the United States and other Schengen nations. But it's vital to know that this 90-day window covers all of Schengen, not just Iceland, and that the timer begins to run upon initial admission into any Schengen nation.

## Passport Validity - Your Key to Iceland

The validity of the travel document is crucial for entry into Iceland. No of their nationality, all travelers must have a good passport for at least six months after the date they intend to leave the Schengen region. This requirement guarantees easy travel and helps avoid potential issues resulting from a passport that is about to expire or has already expired.

## Sufficient Funds and Return Airline Ticket – A Prerequisite

Entry into Iceland is contingent on financial stability. Travelers must show they have the resources necessary to cover their trip expenses without returning to employment. Further documentation that the passenger intends to depart the country within the permitted timeframe, such as a return plane ticket or other proof of onward travel, must be provided.

## Entry Guidelines for Non-Schengen Residents

The prerequisites for entrance differ slightly for citizens who reside outside of the Schengen region. The passport must be current and have three months remaining on it after the desired entrance date into Iceland. It's also important to remember that depending on the traveler's native nation, a visa might occasionally be necessary.

## Working and studying in Iceland

Special rules exist for people who want to work or study in Iceland. Generally, a residency permit is required if the length of the visit exceeds 90 days. The Icelandic Directorate of Immigration accepts applications for these permits from prospective employees and students.

## Requirements for Citizens of Australia, Canada, Japan, New Zealand, and the USA

The Schengen Agreement makes entering Iceland uncomplicated for visitors from Australia, Canada, Japan, New Zealand, and the USA. For stays of fewer than 90 days, visas are not necessary, although passports must be valid for at least another six months after the intended stay.

## Iceland's Entry Protocol for Other Countries

It is advisable for citizens of nations not previously mentioned to check the official website of the Icelandic Directorate of Immigration for information regarding their particular admission requirements. Travelers can guarantee they meet all requirements before setting out on their tour thanks to the site's detailed information that is personalized to every country.

**Where to Find Further Entry Requirement Information**

Several other websites, in addition to the Icelandic Directorate of Immigration, provide helpful details on Iceland's admission requirements. For instance, the Bureau of Consular Affairs of the U.S. Department of State offers current information on visa requirements and travel warnings. The Travel Centre of the International Air Transport Association (IATA) also provides various data on passport, visa, and health requirements worldwide.

While the Schengen Agreement significantly impacts Iceland's entry requirements, those requirements can change based on your nationality, the reason for your visit, and how long you plan to stay. You may guarantee a smooth admission into this stunning Nordic country by remaining informed and making the necessary preparations.

**Travel Tips: Safety, Health, Currency, and Communications**
Iceland is a remarkable, glacial wonder whose attraction draws travelers from all over the world. However, knowledge of safety procedures, health precautions, current events, and communication quirks is essential to enjoy this experience fully. Travelers should read this chapter to navigate Iceland's distinctive landscapes and cultural quirks successfully.

## Understanding Iceland's Terrain

Knowledge is a traveler's first defense to ensure their safety. Comprehending Iceland's topography and climate is essential to navigate its landscapes successfully. A mountainous and stunning island, Iceland is home to several volcanoes, glaciers, hot springs, and waterfalls. However, there are risks associated with these attractions. The weather is erratic, and the terrain can be difficult.

## Weather Conditions and Preparedness

Iceland endures dramatic weather fluctuations that can drastically shift within a day because of its proximity to the Arctic Circle. It can be sunny one second, and then a strong storm might be approaching. "If you don't like the weather, wait five minutes," is a proverb in Iceland. It is crucial to be ready for these circumstances.

Travelers should have the right attire and equipment to handle a sudden change in the weather. Utilizing materials that insulate and withstand wind and water while layering is essential. Before leaving, always check the weather prediction, but be ready for anything.

## Navigating Volcanic Landscapes

Volcanic activity is rife in Iceland, called the "Land of Fire and Ice." Geysers, hot springs, and lava fields are frequently encountered while exploring. These places present safety dangers in addition to amazing scenery. Visitors must obey the warnings and approved paths surrounding these places. A twisted ankle or worse can happen if you stray off the route in a lava field, and erupting geysers and hot springs can cause severe burns.

## Respecting Glacial and Waterfall Safety

Glaciers and waterfalls are among Iceland's most spectacular natural features. However, visitors must remember that these are strong natural forces and should not undervalue their possible risks. Risks around glaciers include icefall, unexpected collapses, and crevasses. When traveling, consider booking a guided tour with informed and experienced experts about these hazards.

Regarding waterfalls, their surroundings are frequently slick and wet. It's important to wear appropriate footwear and stay away from the edges, as the force of the water may drag someone in.

**Road Safety in Iceland**

Iceland's roadways can be difficult to navigate, particularly in rural areas where gravel roads are frequent and during the winter when they may become ice. Learn about Iceland's road system and the present state of the roads before you head out. The Icelandic Road and Coastal Administration provides real-time road conditions and closures updates.

Keep in mind that driving off-road is prohibited in Iceland. This is done to save the delicate environment, which tire tracks have the potential to destroy forever.

**Iceland's Unique Wildlife**

Despite not being dangerous in the sense of predators, Iceland's wildlife can nevertheless be risky. Sheep frequently and freely cross highways in unpredictable ways. Getting hit by one could cause serious harm, so always be vigilant. The ground above puffin nests near cliffs may be unstable and fall way under a person's weight, which can be dangerous.

## Emergency Planning

It's crucial to know what to do in an emergency. Iceland's national emergency number is 112. It is advised to download the 112 Iceland app so that you may, if necessary, provide emergency services with your position.

## Enjoy Iceland Responsibly

Iceland is a country of sharp contrasts, and while it has stunning vistas, it may also be dangerous. Knowing these risks and being ready is essential for a safe and happy trip. Even when looking for the ideal shot, always heed local advice, heed posted signs, and remember that safety comes first.

By familiarizing yourself with Iceland's unique environment, being prepared for unpredictable weather, respecting the powerful forces of nature, and maintaining road and wildlife safety, you can ensure a safe and memorable trip to the Land of Fire and Ice.

## Iceland's Health Travelers Tips

Iceland offers a rare chance to experience nature in all its untamed and unadulterated glory. Understanding basic health and safety rules is essential to making your experience safe and pleasant. We have gathered some essential information to secure your health and well-being throughout your Icelandic journey.

## Emergency Services: Preparation Is Key

Despite being among the safest in the world, Iceland is not exempt from emergencies, so visitors should be ready. In Iceland, the main emergency number is 112. It gives you access to search and rescue, ambulance services, the fire department, and other emergency services. This number should be saved on your mobile device under "emergency" due to the likelihood of confusion in tense situations.

The Iceland emergency number app is available for those who prefer technology. This app aims to improve communication between users and the emergency services. Pressing the red emergency button will send a text message to the contact center with your GPS location if you find yourself in a dangerous scenario. It's a helpful tool in remote areas without good mobile reception because it can still send your coordinates despite low connectivity.

Additionally, the app has a green check-in feature that lets you confirm your safety several times throughout your journey. Authorities receive your GPS position as a preemptive step and store the last five times you checked in. This function may be essential in inclement weather or if you fail to arrive at a pre-arranged place, setting off the alert for a search and rescue operation.

**Understanding Health and Security Risks**

Although Iceland has a low crime rate, it is important to remain cautious. Passports and other valuables shouldn't be left unattended in public places like nightclubs or locked cars. Remember that when people leave bars and clubs late at night and early in the morning, downtown Reykjavik can be busy and even a little chaotic.

Furthermore, despite its reputation for peace, terrorist groups could still use Europe as a target, so it's critical to be aware of your surroundings and report any suspicious behavior to the authorities. To safeguard your safety and report offenses to the local police, dial 112.

## Medical Assistance and Helplines

It's important to remember that seeking medical assistance in a remote place could take some time owing to physical distances, even with top-notch emergency services. Therefore, medical evacuation insurance is advised, especially if you intend to explore the outdoors.

You can call Landsptali Hospital's emergency room at 543-2000 in case of a medical emergency. Call 575-0505 for dental emergencies, and dial 1770 for after-hours medical needs.

A 24-hour hotline is run by the Icelandic Red Cross at 1717. It offers a safety net for mental health emergencies and aids those experiencing grief, anxiety, terror, sadness, or suicidal thoughts.

## Dealing with Loss and Theft

It might be unsettling to lose items or have them stolen when traveling. You can call Missing & Found at 444 -1000 for information about lost or stolen items. Different phone lines are available for Visa (525-2000), American Express (800-8111), Master Card & Diners Club (533-1400/550-1500) if your credit cards are lost or stolen.

In conclusion, being well-prepared is the key to a successful and safe trip. Ensuring you have the knowledge you need can make your Icelandic vacation less stressful and more memorable.

## Money And Travel Expenses

Adventurers have long found Iceland, the "Land of Ice and Fire," to be a paradise. Although even by European standards, it has a reputation for being pricey due to its magnificent landscapes.

Travelers who want to tour Iceland must be aware of the costs and know how to control spending properly.

## Understanding Iceland's Travel Expenses

Like other Scandinavian nations, Iceland is frequently listed as one of the least economically friendly countries. When planning to travel to Iceland, you should prioritize budgeting for lodging, meals, transportation, and tours.

Travelers can anticipate spending between 9,000 and 10,000 ISK daily at the very least. This spending plan considers taking public transportation, camping or staying in hostels, going on free excursions, preparing all of one's meals (dining out might be expensive), and drinking far less alcohol.

However, a mid-range budget of 23,000 ISK a day could allow for sporadic cheap dining out, the occasional beer, car rentals (if the expense can be split), and more costly activities like museum visits.

Luxury passengers should budget at least 36,000 ISK each day. This spending limit permits staying in cheap lodgings, dining out often, taking trips, renting a car, and having fun on date nights.

## Tips on Cutting Expenses in Iceland

Planning your trip early is one of the best ways to save expenses. You may generally acquire the services at reduced charges if you plan ahead1. Here are some tried-and-true suggestions to assist you in cutting costs on your trip:

1. **Self-Cooked Meals**: Icelandic restaurants are very pricey, with a basic one-course menu frequently costing between 30

and 45 USD. As a result, cooking your meals can help you save a lot of money. Bringing snacks from home can also help you avoid getting hungry while traveling.

2. **Accommodation Planning**: Consider options like hostels, camping, or Airbnb instead of choosing pricey hotels. Sharing lodging with other travelers might also help you save a lot of money.

3. **Hitchhiking and Carpooling**: One of the safest countries for hitchhikers is Iceland. Since petrol is expensive and many tourists use the main ring road (M1), they typically don't mind picking you up if you can chip in for gas.

4. **Enjoy Free Attractions**: With innumerable waterfalls, hiking paths, and mountains to explore, Iceland has abundant natural beauty. Iceland's natural attractions are generally free to visit except for a few parking sites that demand a fair fee.

5. **Limit Alcohol Consumption**: Icelandic alcohol is infamously costly. Your everyday expenses can be significantly decreased by limiting or eliminating alcohol.

It's crucial to remember that "cheap" has a different definition in this stunning European nation while planning your travel budget to Iceland. However, you can take advantage of Iceland's offers without exceeding your budget if you prepare and are careful with your money. After all, Iceland's breathtaking scenery, which is its best feature, is free.

A Window into Iceland's Culture and Heritage: The Icelandic Language

The use of the Icelandic language is one fascinating part of Icelandic culture and tradition. Most Icelanders speak Icelandic, a North Germanic language also spoken in Canada, the United States, Denmark, Norway, and Sweden. Despite having close relations to Norwegian and Faroese, Icelandic stands out thanks to its distinctive characteristics that have been carefully preserved.

The Icelandic Language Committee merits praise for preserving Icelandic authenticity throughout history. The group puts a lot of work into protecting the language and fending off outside influences. The official Icelandic alphabet has several unusual letters that are missing from the English alphabet, such as the letter "á" (pronounced like the English word "eye") and the letters "orn" and " that stand for the voiceless and voiced "th" sounds, respectively.

Even though English and other languages are widely spoken in Iceland, learning even a little Icelandic can tremendously improve your travels and show that you respect the locals. As a result, this chapter gives you access to crucial Icelandic words, phrases, and translations.

Basic Icelandic greetings and phrases

**Icelandic English Translation**

Já Yes Nei No Takk Thank you Takk fyrir Thank you very much.

Þú ert velkominn/Gerðu svo vel You're welcome.

Vinsamlegast/Takk Please

Fyrirgefðu Excuse me

Halló/Góðan daginn Hello Bless Goodbye

Hvað heitir þú? What is your name?

Gaman að kynnast þér Nice to meet you

Hvernig hefur þú það? How are you?

Góður/Góð Good

Vondur/Vond Bad.

Language & Communication:

**Icelandic English Translation**

Talar þú ensku? Do you speak English?

Ég skil ekki, I don't understand

Hvað þýðir þetta? What does this mean?

Getur þú talað hægar? Can you speak slower?

Ég tala ekki íslensku I don't speak Icelandic

Directions:

**Icelandic English Translation**

Hvar er...? Where is...?

Vinstri Left Hægri Right

Beint áfram Straight ahead

Kort Map

Transportation:

**Icelandic English Translation**

Flugvöllur Airport

Strætó (bus) Bus Lest Train

Bílaleiga Car rental

Hvar er næsta stöð? Where is the next stop?

Eating & Drinking:

**Icelandic English Translation**

Matur Food

Drykkur Drink

Veitingastaður Restaurant

Ég er vegan/vegetarískur I am vegan/vegetarian

Gæti ég fengið vatn, takk? Could I have some water, please?

Accommodation:

**Icelandic English Translation**

Hótel Hotel

Herbergi Room

Frí Vacancy Ég hef bókað herbergi I have a reservation

Shopping & Money:

**Icelandic English Translation**

Verslun Shop

Hversu mikið kostar þetta? How much does this cost?

Ég vil kaupa þetta I want to buy this

Kreditkort Credit card Peningar Money

Sightseeing:

**Icelandic English Translation**

Áhugaverður staður Interesting place

Miðaldaborg Medieval castle Fjall Mountain

Jökull Glacier Eyja Island

Basic Numbers:

**Icelandic English Translation**

Núll Zero

Einn One

Tveir Two

Þrír Three

Fjórir Four

Fimm Five

Sex Six

Sjö Seven

Átta Eight

Níu Nine

Tíu Ten

Your trip will certainly be enhanced by being familiar with and using these fundamental Icelandic words and phrases. Although complicated vocabulary is frequently utilized, it's crucial to remember that Icelandic pronunciation prioritizes words' first syllables. Although it could need some getting used to, this trait will also help to make your trip more enjoyable.

When traveling to Iceland, it's important to consider the numerous communication channels and indispensable travel apps available. Here are some suggestions to make your travel easier:

1. **Mobile Connectivity**: Consider your carrier's international data plans if you're traveling from the US; they can be a more affordable choice. Customers of Sprint and T-Mobile now have completely free options. However, AT&T and Verizon may need to watch out for hefty data charges. If your phone supports this function, you might also consider installing an eSIM, a virtual SIM, on your unlocked phone. Additionally, it's important to know that physical SIM card slots are becoming less common, especially on some of the newest gadgets like the iPhone 14. Major Icelandic cell phone providers, including Sminn, Nova, and Vodafone, provide services for a local choice.

2. **Wi-Fi Access**: In Iceland, public areas, including hotels, eateries, bookstores, bars, and cafés typically have free Wi-Fi. Wi-Fi may be offered in even the most isolated, small villages and gas stations. However, there may be a small price. You might also consider hiring a mobile Wi-Fi hotspot, which might be useful if you need to stay connected or get lost and find your way back.

3. **Useful Apps**: There are numerous apps created especially for Iceland travelers. The Icelandic Meteorological Office's Veur app, which offers real-time updates on weather conditions, news, weather predictions, and hazard warnings, is essential. Facebook Messenger, Snapchat, Instagram, and Google Maps are additional helpful apps for communication and navigation.

4. **Emergency Services**: Additionally, it's critical to have emergency phone numbers handy. In Iceland, dial 112 if there is a crisis.

5. **Keeping Informed**: Visit the official tourism information page or hire a local tour guide for up-to-date, factual information on Iceland.

Ensure your phone is unlocked, prepare your gadgets for overseas travel by enabling roaming services if necessary, and pack a power adaptor that can be used in Iceland.

Happy travels!

# Chapter 2: Top Attractions

**Exploring Reykjavík: The Vibrant Capital of Iceland**

Considering that you're interested in visiting Reykjavik, the energetic capital of Iceland, here are some additional sights and activities you might enjoy:

1. **Aurora Reykjavik: The Northern Lights Center**: Anyone interested in the Aurora Borealis, or Northern Lights, must go to this location. This distinctive exhibit offers a historical and academic viewpoint on this natural occurrence. This location offers an educational experience for kids and adults, with interactive exhibits and even VR headsets to view the aurora.

2. **The Saga Museum - Sogusafnid**: Consider going to the Saga Museum if you want to learn everything there is to know about Iceland's past. Learn about the earliest settlers and understand Iceland's past through lifelike wax models of

historical figures and significant events. Additionally, the museum offers an audio tour that tells tales as you pass the displays.

3. **The Icelandic Punk Museum**: Visit the Icelandic Punk Museum if you're a fan of music, especially punk. The museum in the heart of Reykjavik exhibits the history of Iceland's punk culture, from its inception until the new wave rebellion. Here, you may discover how this musical style affected some of the country's most well-known performers, such as Bjork and Sigur Ros.

Visitors have also appreciated other fascinating and educational museums, according to recommendations made by travelers on TripAdvisor, albeit precise names are not given in the report. Reviews, however, indicate that some are concentrated on subjects like glaciers, Icelandic structures, fishing history, and science exhibits with humor.

Remember that there are more than 60 museums, galleries, and exhibition halls in Reykjavik. Whether interested in history, art, nature, or literature, the city's dedication to the arts and culture offers you a wide range of options.

### The Golden Circle Region: Þingvellir, Geysir, and Gullfoss

The Golden Circle route in Iceland is a breathtakingly gorgeous drive that passes by some of the most well-known locations in the nation, including Ingvellir National Park, the Geysir Geothermal Area, and Gullfoss Waterfall. It is a must-see adventure for all tourists. These locations highlight Iceland's spectacular beauty and intriguing geology.

**Þingvellir National Park**: Ingvellir National Park, a UNESCO World Heritage site, is renowned for its breathtaking scenery and deep cultural heritage. The Aling General Assembly, the oldest surviving parliament, held its first meeting here in 930 A.D. The park's location on the Mid-Atlantic Ridge, a tectonic plate boundary that divides the Eurasian and North American plates, makes for intriguing geology. It is the only location on Earth where it can stand between two continental plates on dry land. The largest natural lake in Iceland, Ingvallavatn, and various other animals may be found in the national park.

**Geysir Geothermal Area**: One of the rare locations on Earth where you may see active geysers is Haukadalur. The Great Geysir and Strokkur geysers are the most well-known; the latter typically erupts every 8 to 10 minutes, spewing boiling water up to 30 meters into the air.

**Gullfoss Waterfall**: Awe-inspiring scenery may be seen at Gullfoss, one of Iceland's most famous waterfalls, as glacial water from the Hvtá River plunges 31 meters into the Gullfossgljfur canyon. The waterfall continues to be a clean aesthetic joy because of the conservation efforts of Sigrur Tómasdóttir, an Icelandic conservation hero.

You may want to think about stopping at other local attractions like the medieval Bishop's See Skálholt and the volcanic crater Keri while touring the Golden Circle road. Visit one of the area's many geothermal pools and greenhouses if you're curious about geothermal energy. Everyone will find something to enjoy in the Golden Circle's many offers, whether they are history buffs, geology enthusiasts, or wildlife lovers. Enjoy your trip to this amazing area!

## Glacier Adventures: Exploring Vatnajökull Glacier and Its Wonders

Experience a surreal sight in an alabaster country where time seems to stand still, and regular landscapes take on strange qualities. Welcome to Vatnajökull Glacier, a place of unimaginable glacial magnificence.

**Navigating the Icy Terrain**

Put the crampons on, and start your expedition. Set out on an energizing hike over Europe's largest ice cap while closely supervised by knowledgeable guides. These unbroken white stretches of ice are a wonder to behold and a privilege to traverse. Be lured further and deeper into the icy splendor of Vatnajökull with each step. You will be in amazement by the variety of ice formations, some as transparent as a polished diamond and others as blue as the deepest ocean.

A symphony of crackles and pops breaks the ice's stillness, creating a mesmerizing melody of melting ice reverberating across the glacial wilderness. As you explore, learn about the science underlying these formations, how these enormous structures have changed Iceland's landscapes, and how they are currently coping with the unrelenting effects of climate change.

**Journey into the Heart of the Glacier: The Ice Caves**

Explore the ice caves' otherworldly splendor by going further inside the glacier. These captivating chambers, sculpted by the forces of nature, are an ever-evolving work of art. The icy walls enclose the vast space, which creates a scene of stunning blues and glistening whites. It is impossible to describe the atmosphere produced by the beams of sunshine that pass through the frozen façade other than as magical.

## The Expanse Beyond: Vatnajökull National Park

Once you've filled the glacial wonders, let the allure of the surrounding Vatnajökull National Park draw you in. Venture off the icy path and into a verdant paradise adorned with stunning glacial valleys that echo the whispers of age-old sagas. Encounter the resilient flora and fauna that call this place home, adding a vibrant splash of color and life to the icy backdrop.

Marvel at the spectacle of glacial rivers carving their way through the park's landscape. These mighty waterways, powered by the glacier, create a dynamic spectacle as they shape and reshape the landscape in a dance as old as time.

An expedition to the heart of Vatnajökull Glacier and its surroundings is no ordinary trek; it's an extraordinary odyssey that takes you into the very soul of Iceland. Whether you're an adventure enthusiast, a nature lover, or simply someone searching for the spectacular, this glacial adventure is worth taking.

## The South Coast: Waterfalls, Black Sand Beaches, and Dramatic Cliffs

The south coast of Iceland is home to the largest glacier in Europe and serves as the entrance to some of the most beautiful hiking locations in the nation. It also boasts an astounding array of waterfalls, glaciers, and well-known black-sand beaches. From Hvolsvöllur to Höfn, the area tucked away along the Ring Road reveals a wealth of breathtaking natural wonders that captivate tourists.

### The Mesmerizing Waterfalls

Each magnificent waterfall along Iceland's south coast is more beautiful than the last. Seljalandsfoss and Gljfrabi, conveniently accessible to the Ring Road, are at the top of the list.

At about 60 meters high, Seljalandsfoss is a rare example of a waterfall. Visitors can view this natural wonder from a unique vantage point along a trail behind the waterfall, giving an amazing experience. The view from behind is utterly enthralling, especially on sunny days when a rainbow adds to the charm, even though the path can be slick in the winter and caution is always advised.

Gljfrabi, often called "Dweller in the Gorge," is not far from Seljalandsfoss, tucked away in a gorge. Gljfrabi's appeal rests in its hidden beauty, despite being partially blocked by a big rock. This waterfall, which is 40 meters high, is accessible to visitors, giving them a close-up view of the majesty and force of nature.

## Black Sand Beaches and Dramatic Cliffs

As much as its ice-covered stretches, Iceland's south coast's black sand beaches serve as a symbol of its distinctive landscape. Reynisfjara Beach is well-known for its expansive black beaches, impressive basalt columns, and recognizable Reynisdrangar sea stacks. It is located close to the town of Vk Mrdal.

A stunning arch of black lava that extends into the sea is guarded by the Dyrhólaey Lighthouse farther along the beach. This location is excellent for birdwatching since it provides views of puffins and other marine birds while they are nesting.

## Glaciers and Glacier Lagoons

Without taking in the magnificence of Vatnajökull, Europe's largest glacier, and the captivating Jökulsárlón Glacier Lagoon, no trip to the south coast is complete1. The area offers a singular opportunity to get close to these frozen wonders, with activities ranging from glacier walks and ice cave excursions to boat and kayak cruises maneuvering between tiny icebergs at the Fjallsárlón and Jökulsárlón lagoons.

Hikers will find paradise at the Vatnajökull National Park, home to Hvannadalshnjkur, Iceland's highest peak. It has several breathtakingly beautiful locales and various hiking trails with varied degrees of difficulty.

**The Local Flavor: Lighthouses, Lobsters, and Museums**

The South Coast's little communities offer intriguing gastronomic gems and cultural insights. The South Coast Lighthouse Trail, which includes órlákshöfn, Eyrarbakki, and Stokkseyr, mixes the appeal of lighthouses with outdoor pursuits, mouthwatering seafood, and tranquil walks by the shore.

The langoustine, a species of little lobster, is a gourmet treat for connoisseurs. Restaurants around the south coast provide a wide variety of delectable langoustine dishes. The culinary tour of the south coast ends in Höfn, recognized as Iceland's lobster capital.

The south coast of Iceland offers a remarkable journey into the heart of a unique landscape with its blend of natural beauties and cultural highlights. Whether you're an explorer, a nature lover, or a foodie, this area guarantees once-in-a-lifetime experiences.

### Snæfellsnes Peninsula: Mountains, Volcanoes, and Coastal Charm

The Snfellsnes Peninsula offers numerous opportunities to experience mesmerizing Icelandic landscapes. The peninsula is home to abundant natural wonders just waiting to be discovered, from its recognizable mountains to its charming coastline charm.

## The Exquisite Charm of Kirkjufell & Kirkjufellsfoss

The magnificent Kirkjufell, often known as "Church Mountain," is situated on the peninsula's northern coast and is about 1,520 feet tall. This magnificent mountain is the most popular natural wonder to be photographed in Iceland because of its distinctive conical shape and seaside location. Due to its significant appearance in the well-known television series "Game of Thrones," it has also attracted notice on a global scale.

The Kirkjufellsfoss waterfall, with its glistening waters, is located close to Kirkjufell. When the sun sets, the mountain and the glistening waterfall are illuminated, providing an unmatched viewing experience that makes for the ideal setting for photos. The area is also renowned for its breathtaking Northern Lights displays, making it a stargazer's paradise.

## The Historic Fishing Villages of Arnarstapi and Hellnar

Explore the historic fishing communities of Arnarstapi and Hellnar amid Snfellsjökull National Park. These little towns, situated at the base of the Snfellsjökull glacier, provide a fascinating look into the inhabitants' traditional way of life and Iceland's vibrant marine tradition.

These communities' allure transcends their historical importance. They offer the perfect backdrop for nature enthusiasts, photographers, and adventurers due to the breathtaking scenery surrounding them. Visitors can experience Iceland's different ecosystems by strolling along the shoreline between Arnarstapi and Hellnar, which offers a lovely trail of strange rock formations, caves, and bird colonies.

**Journeying through Snæfellsjökull National Park**

The Snfellsjökull National Park, which bears the glacier's name, is breathtaking. The Skardsvk Beach with its black sand, the secluded Svortuloft and Ndverdarnes lighthouses, the Saxhóll Crater, and the breathtaking Londrangar2 basalt cliffs are just a few of the attractions in this area. The park showcases the unadulterated beauty of Iceland's landscapes by offering an eclectic mix of geology and geographic elements.

Visit Djpalónssandur Beach, renowned for its black pebbles and fascinating iron shipwreck artifacts. A must-see is the Vatnshellir Cave, where you can learn more about Iceland's volcanic past.

**Navigating the Peninsula**

It is an experience just to go through the Snfellsnes Peninsula. You can go directly through a tunnel beneath the water or take a leisurely detour off Highway 1 based on your preferences. You'll be rewarded in either case with stunning views and distinctive sceneries.

Renting a car is advised if you want to explore the peninsula at your own pace. However, Reykjavik offers many trip alternatives for individuals who prefer guided excursions. Whatever route you choose, the Snfellsnes Peninsula guarantees a spectacular journey through some of Iceland's most beautiful landscapes.

So, are you prepared to explore the Snfellsnes Peninsula's vivacious charm?

### The Far North: Akureyri, Mývatn, and Nature's Wonders

For any discriminating visitor, a trip to Iceland's far north—a region rich in untouched landscapes and unique geological phenomena—remains a must. This chapter explores Akureyri, Lake Mvatn, and the breathtaking natural features that define these fascinating locations.

## Akureyri: Gateway to the North

The "Capital of the North," Akureyri, is a city with a warm yet energetic vibe close to the Arctic Circle. It provides a lovely home base for visiting the nearby natural attractions, with the spectacular backdrop of snow-capped mountains. The lovely city also offers a variety of attractions, such as art galleries, botanical gardens, and local cafés where craft beers and traditional Icelandic food can be enjoyed.

## Lake Mývatn: The Diamond Circle's Crown Jewel

The northernmost lake in the nation, Lake Mvatn, is well known for its distinctive geology, a plethora of bird life, and thermal springs.

Remember to bring your mosquito repellant throughout the summer since its name is "Midge Lake."

The region around the lake is similarly captivating, featuring lava fields, volcanic craters, and geothermal sites. Dimmuborgir, a labyrinth of enormous lava pillars and arches engraved by millennia of wind and water erosion, is one of the area's most well-known attractions.

### The Bustling Life of Reykjahlíð

The charming town of Reykjahl is located on the banks of Lake Mvatn. It is the perfect location for rest and exploration due to its tranquil surroundings and proximity to the lake's attractions. The town's essential amenities include hotels, cafes, and a medical facility. There are so many adventures right outside your door, from the mesmerizing Mvatn Nature Baths to the breathtaking scenery of the Krafla volcano.

### The Diamond Circle: A Route of Remarkable Wonders

The hamlet of Hsavk, the canyon of Sbyrgi, the waterfall of Dettifoss, and Lake Mvatn are all included in the renowned viewing circuit known as the Diamond Circle. Hsavk, dubbed the hub of whale watching in Europe, enchants tourists with its bustling harbor and breathtaking panoramas of the Skjálfandi sea.

The history of the horseshoe-shaped valley known as Sbyrgi Canyon is fascinating. It is thought to have developed when Sleipnir, Odin's eight-legged horse, contacted the earth. The Hljóaklettar rock formations are nearby, a spectacular display of basalt columns extending in all directions.

The most potent waterfall in Europe, Dettifoss, cascades into an eerie, dark gorge, offering a spectacular display of strength and beauty. Goafoss, often known as "the waterfall of the gods," is a nearby waterfall so named because of its historical importance to Icelandic Christianity.

## Unforgettable Tours: Experience the Magic

Start a day trip to the Diamond Circle from Akureyri to see the breathtaking sights in a short amount of time. This is the ideal method to take in the classic sights if you only have a short time in the area. Anyone interested in learning more about each location might easily spend a week taking in the sights in and around Mvatn.

Godafoss, Dettifoss, and Selfoss waterfalls, the Dimmuborgir lava fields, hot springs, and the geothermal lagoon at Myvatn Nature Baths are all included in the journey. An exploration-filled day can be finished with a plunge in the naturally heated lagoon.

## Námaskarð Pass: A Geothermal Wonderland

On Mount Námafjall, the Námaskar Pass is a geothermal wonder begging to be discovered. The tremendous geothermal activity beneath the Earth's surface has created bubbling mud pots, steaming fumaroles, and vividly colored clay. This region serves as a sharp reminder of the erratic forces that produced this gorgeous country, starkly contrasting Iceland's verdant landscapes.

You will see the magnificent scope of Mother Nature's creation as you travel across Iceland's far north. Every place reveals a distinct aspect of the country's extraordinary character, from the resounding thunder of waterfalls to the tranquil beauty of Lake Mvatn. These are, in fact, the locations where myths come to life, and the untamed elements of nature are in full force.

### The Highlands: Untouched Landscapes and Wild Adventures

The Icelandic Highlands are a veritable treasure trove of unspoiled natural beauty. It hides some of Iceland's best-kept secrets because it is a rough and wild area frequently missed by the typical tourist route. The Highlands, which are in the middle of the country and make up most of Iceland's landmass, are generally inaccessible and uninhabited. Their natural terrain, carved by canyons and shaped by volcanic activity, provides a singular excursion into Iceland's wildness.

But getting to this hilly region requires a challenging hike along the notorious Iceland f-roads, which avoids the well-maintained Ring Road. The need for a 4x4 vehicle on this unpaved, difficult terrain adds to the experience's adventure and excitement. The landlocked Icelandic Highlands can be safely explored via guided trips for people hesitant to cross this treacherous terrain.

### Landmannalaugar: A Painted Landscape

The Fjallabak Nature Reserve's Landmannalaugar is a portion of the Icelandic Highlands and one of its most famous destinations. The region's volcanic activity has produced some of the most breathtaking vistas in the nation, distinguished by various hues. The Brennisteinsalda volcano is a striking illustration of this area's geothermal vigor, with its acid yellows, mossy greens, ash blues, and streaks of black from the lava.

But Landmannalaugar's fame isn't just due to its volcanic activity. It is the location of Hekla, the island's most active volcano, and some of Iceland's top hot springs. The most well-known hiking routes in Landmannalaugar are the 32-mile Laugavegur path to Thórsmörk and the shorter 3.7-mile Bláhnkur route to Iceland's blue peak. A trip to Landmannalaugar is a sensory extravaganza that offers a singular experience.

## Aldeyjarfoss and Langjokull Glacier: Captivating Wonders

Aldeyjarfoss, a 65-foot waterfall on the Skjalfandafljot River known for its magnificent basalt columns and a sizable pool, is another noteworthy location in the Highlands. Photographers who want to capture the breathtaking Icelandic scenery now favor it.

Another important site nearby is Langjokull, often known as the "Long Glacier". The greatest way to experience Iceland's second-largest glacier is on a guided trip. Exciting methods to cross this enormous glacier include hiking, snowmobiling, and riding in a giant Jeep. Winter travel offers the rare chance to explore manufactured ice tunnels that reach 500 meters into the glacier and naturally occurring ice caves with spectacular colors and patterns.

## Þórsmörk: A Hiker's Dream

One of Iceland's most well-liked hiking locations is órsmörk, a natural reserve tucked away between three glaciers: Eyjafjallajökull, Mrdalsjökull, and Tindafjallajökull. This valley features contrasted terrain with white rivers meandering through black desert sands and oasis of moss, fern, and birchwood, all surrounded by ice-capped mountain slopes shrouded in lovely mist.

Some of Iceland's most incredible hiking trails can be found on the terrain around órsmörk, such as the 30 km Fimmvorduhals trail, which leads into the craggy hills beneath the Eyjafjallajökull glacier volcano, and the 55 km Laugavegur trail, which departs from órsmörk and travels into the breathtaking Landmannalaugar region.

## The Volcano Hekla: The Gateway to Hell

Hekla, one of the planet's most active volcanoes and an important component of the Highlands' geological and cultural history, must be brought up while discussing the Icelandic Highlands. This fiery marvel has erupted more than twenty times since Iceland was settled and spawned innumerable stories and legends. The intriguing and dynamic scenery of the Icelandic Highlands is still being shaped by the ash and lava of Hekla, formerly thought to be a portal to hell.

You may experience Iceland's wild, untamed beauty by exploring the Icelandic Highlands on your own or as part of a guided tour. The Highlands, which offer an unparalleled excursion into the untamed landscapes and wild adventures that Iceland promises, symbolize the country's wild heart with its astounding geological characteristics, nature reserves, and hiking paths.

# Chapter 3: Experiences and Activities

## Glacier Hiking: Trekking and Snowy Adventures

Iceland, often known as the Land of Ice and Fire, is shrouded in mystery and majesty and attracts tourists with its beautiful scenery. The nation's glaciers, one of its numerous attractions, possess a grandeur, whispering tales of ages past and luring the daring. One of the most memorable activities one can partake in in this Nordic country is hiking a glacier, which combines excitement with a deep understanding of the incredible creativity of nature.

## Why Choose Glacier Hiking in Iceland?

Despite being compared to activities like riding Icelandic horses or diving between two tectonic plates, glacier hiking in Iceland has a certain charm. Drinking pure glacial water gives your experience an authentic touch as the sound of the ice under your feet reverberates in the vast quiet. As you travel over the immense ice fields, there are starkly visible signs of our planet's ongoing change.

**Stepping onto the Glacial Expanse: What to Expect**

It is fascinating to participate in a glacier hike in Iceland. Standing atop the enormous Vatnajökull Glacier is breathtaking or looking out over the expanse of ice from Sólheimajökull Glacier. Contrary to popular belief, this exercise is not necessarily physically taxing. Yes, crossing the ice can be done carefully and deliberately. This should not, however, lessen the awe that one must feel at the wonder of the glaciers or the need for caution when making such a journey.

**Choosing Your Glacier: Sólheimajökull and Vatnajökull**

Sólheimajökull and Vatnajökull are the two glaciers in Iceland that people most frequently hike on. Many tourists favor Sólheimajökull because of its convenient location in southern Iceland, close to the Skógafoss waterfall and only two hours from Reykjavik. It is ideal for day getaways or as a stop on a south coast tour.

For those with a greater sense of adventure, Vatnajökull, the largest glacier in Europe and a component of Vatnajökull National Park, offers an incredible alternative. About 30 outlet glaciers can be found there, some prominently depicted in the television show Game of Thrones.

**The Living Ice: Understanding Glaciers**

Understanding how glaciers grow can help hikers appreciate their trip more. In areas where snow accumulates over time, glaciers are born. The pressure on the layers below rises with the height of the snow, which causes ice to form. Unlike what is commonly believed, glaciers are always moving, albeit very slowly. The glacier is pushed downhill by gravity forces and the weight of the ice, changing the terrain over time.

**Safety First: Preparing for Your Iceland Glacier Hike**

It's not a decision to be made lightly to venture onto a glacier. Although the calm ice can seem innocuous, it's important to remember that glaciers always move. Every day can bring new changes to the ice, caves, and ecology. Professional guides are essential for a secure and pleasurable trip. These professionals conduct daily surveys of the area to identify suitable trails, monitor weather predictions, and guarantee hikers' safety. Due to potential risks, it is strongly advised against hiking glaciers in Iceland without qualified supervision.

**Capturing the Experience: Tours and More**

The glacier trekking experience can be customized to your interests, thanks to the availability of guided tours. There are many possibilities, whether you're interested in a quick or lengthy stroll, an intense ice climbing session, or a trip to an ice cave. The possibility of exploring naturally occurring ice caves with blue ice ceilings throughout the winter months gives the encounter a mystical touch. Whatever you decide, the voyage will undoubtedly leave you with memories that last long after you've left the frozen wastes behind.

Icelandic glacier hiking is a magnificent activity that skillfully combines calmness, awe, excitement, and a deepened appreciation for the unadulterated beauty of nature. This unique excursion guarantees a glimpse into civilization as old as time and as fascinating as its legends. So arm yourself against the elements, enjoy the chill, and listen to the glaciers' icy words.

## Thermal Nature: Iceland's Hot Springs and Geothermal Pools

Geothermal phenomena create an incredible scene of bubbling hot springs, naturally heated pools, and plumes of steam that whisper tales of the earth's inner unrest in Iceland, a country where fire meets ice. Because Icelanders have mastered using these geothermal resources, the nation now boasts an astounding variety of hot springs and geothermal pools.

## The Science Behind the Scenery

The Mid-Atlantic Rift, which lies beneath Iceland's rough terrain and permits magma to ascend, creates the ideal circumstances for volcanic activity. This underground inferno heats water trapped in the earth's crust, resulting in hot springs when the water rises to the surface. On the other hand, the warmth of geothermal pools results from a more intentional human intervention that uses Iceland's abundant geothermal energy to heat these well-liked swimming facilities.

## Where to Take the Plunge: Iceland's Top Geothermal Spots

The numerous naturally heated pools and hot springs dot the Icelandic landscape and serve inhabitants and visitors, each with a distinct flair.

### Reykjarfjarðarlaug (The Westfjords)

The geothermal springs of Reykjarfjararlaug tucked away at the head of Reykjarfjörur, offer stunning views of the fjord, mountains, and soaring seabirds. The major draw is a natural, turf-fringed pool with water heated to a pleasant 45°C. A concrete pool up front gives way to it.

### Krossneslaug (The Westfjords)

On an untamed black-pebble beach, Krossneslaug, a geothermal infinity pool and hot tub, is perched at the apex of the universe. The view from this pool of the dancing waves and the midnight sun is unmatched and should not be missed.

### Sundhöll Reykjavíkur (Reykjavík)

The oldest pool in Reykjavik, Sundhöllin, features an indoor pool and an updated outdoor space that includes hot tubs, a sauna, and a swimming pool. A fantastic vantage point for city views is an upper hot tub.

### Bláa Lónið/The Blue Lagoon (Reykjanes Peninsula)

The Blue Lagoon's azure waters create an almost unearthly environment in a black lava field. The skin is nourished by the superheated water supplied by the Svartsengi geothermal plant, which is rich in blue-green algae, mineral salts, and fine silica mud.

### Krauma (Reykholt, West Iceland)

The largest hot spring in Iceland, Deildartunguhver, supplies the water for Krauma's contemporary outdoor bathing facility. Five multi-temperature hot pots, two steam baths, and a cold tub plunge are available for guests.

### The Cultural Impact of Geothermal Bathing

The practice of geothermal bathing is fundamental to Icelandic culture. The fact that almost every town has at least one heated swimming pool, or "sundlaug," which is frequently located outside, shows how highly the country values its thermal resources. Locals gather for this social gathering to unwind and enjoy some humorous conversation. However, using these natural pools for bathing requires a strict code of cleanliness, which calls for careful pre-entry washing.

## Conclusion: An Elemental Embrace

Iceland embraces its natural heritage and invites visitors to experience its alluring hot springs and geothermal pools. These aren't just locations for fun; they provide a fascinating look at the nation's changeable geology. They also add to Iceland's appeal by luring tourists looking for comfort in the warm embrace of these naturally heated waters. It is an immersive experience to visit Iceland's hot springs and geothermal pools, which capture the untamed beauty and amazing geothermal force of this "Land of Ice and Fire."

## Whale Watching: Encounters with Majestic Sea Giants

Whales have played a significant role in Icelandic culture and history to the point where the word "hvalreki," which refers to a lucky break, literally means "beached whale." Today, whale viewing is a must-do activity on any vacation to Iceland, just like seeing the northern lights, hot springs, and glaciers. These gentle ocean giants are now adored from afar.

## The Best Time for Whale Encounters

In Iceland, whale viewing is possible all year, but May through September is the most popular. Because migrating whales use Iceland's fertile coasts as a feeding area, the summer months, especially June to August, give the best opportunities for observing pods. During this time, one can have unusual experiences like seeing these amazing creatures under the midnight sun. Even though it's chilly and the seas can be choppy, winter has its special beauty thanks to the snow-covered mountains, the sunsets, and perhaps even the chance to see the Northern Lights.

## Diversity in the Deep

The Icelandic territorial waters offer a diverse and abundant feeding area that draws 24 distinct whale species, including the huge sperm whale and the small harbor porpoise, thanks to a rare combination of cold and warm marine currents and plenty of summer daylight.

Depending on the port of departure, a whale-watching trip's chances of seeing a particular whale species vary. For instance, the minke whale can be observed all year round in Iceland despite being a very shy animal and being abundant.

## Whales and More: The Majestic Marine Life

One can see white-beaked dolphins, seals, occasionally basking sharks and numerous whale species. Boat tours are rich in biodiversity and a feast for the senses since they provide a fantastic opportunity to see seabirds like puffins, gannets, gulls, and arctic terns in their feeding grounds.

## Whale Watching Hotspots

There are whale-watching tours offered all across Iceland. For instance, Reykjavik makes whale watching accessible, with the ocean only a short stroll from the city center. Travel to Faxaflói Bay, a well-known location where humpback and minke whales, white-beaked dolphins, and occasionally orcas can be seen.

Due to the high viewing rates in this area, a trip north will reward whale watchers with a variety of whales. Only the north of Iceland can boast of having seen all 24 species of whales known to live in Iceland's seas. On a traditional whale-watching excursion, the fishing village of Hsavk, known as Europe's "whale viewing capital," promises sights close to Skjálfandi Bay.

**Ensuring Ethical Encounters**

It has become crucial to respect the habitats of the animals as whale watching has become increasingly popular. To guarantee that these marine giants continue to flourish in their natural habitat, Iceland's whale-watching tour providers must abide by strict conduct regulations.

Icelandic seas are home to various marine species, and whale watching provides a rare opportunity to see these amazing animals in their native environment. Every journey offers a fresh opportunity to experience these gigantic sea giants' mesmerizing exhibition, leaving behind lifelong memories.

## Trekking and Excursions: Exploring Panoramic Trails and Nature Reserves

The Hornstrandir Nature Reserve, perched on the northernmost point of the Westfjords, is a witness to Iceland's untainted beauty. Hornstrandir, one of Europe's last remaining real wildernesses, is a haven for hikers and nature lovers with its beautiful mosaic of towering mountains, jagged cliffs, and intricate network of fjords.

The ferry voyage from the busy town of Safjörur to Hornstrandir adds an element of adventure to your journey. The Royal Horn, a four- to five-day trip highlighting the variety of Hornstrandir's scenery, is the most well-known trekking path. You'll go over high mountain passes, take in the beauty of falling waterfalls, come across a deserted settlement, and come across glacial fjords. This trek lets you see the reserve's unique environment, home to various creatures, including the Arctic fox, seals, and other bird species.

The landscapes of Hornstrandir can be thoroughly explored on guided trips, which are ideal for novice hikers or those looking for a planned adventure. These excursions provide you with the instruction and equipment required to enjoy the difficult terrain of the reserve safely.

**Gearing Up for Your Trekking Adventure in Iceland**

Icelandic hiking takes careful planning, especially in places like Hornstrandir. Every little thing counts, from choosing the appropriate gear to taking the trek's technical aspects into account. Your hike will be made more difficult by the fast weather changes in Iceland. You'll need sturdy footwear, warm clothing, and wind- and waterproof coats to stay comfortable throughout your excursion.

Planning your trip also entails knowing how far and how long the hike will take and the kind of terrain you can expect. It is strongly advised to have a hiking map, either physical or digital, as it not only assists with navigating but also with planning the remaining portions of the journey.

The availability of drinking water along most Icelandic treks' routes is one of their benefits. Bringing a refillable water bottle on a walk is standard procedure. Bringing energy-boosting snacks is also crucial to stay fuelled while hiking.

**The Mesmerizing Trails of Þórsmörk Nature Reserve**

The órsmörk Nature Reserve is a must-see for hikers seeking a fusion of volcanic scenery, glaciers, and valleys. It provides some of Iceland's most varied and stunning trails. The Volcano Huts make a cozy basecamp, and the paths in órsmörk are ideal for hiking and trail running.

The órsgata Trail, which runs between the famous Laugavegur and Fimmvöruháls paths, is the most well-traveled route in this reserve. Depending on your pace and preferences, it offers a diverse selection of trekking experiences that can be accomplished over several days.

The órsmörk Panorama and órsmörk Highlights circles offer a condensed version of the best the reserve has to offer for a quick but rewarding hike. These routes lead you through some of the reserve's most beautiful areas, providing panoramic vistas and a rich, varied understanding of Iceland's natural world.

Icelandic trekking is an engaging activity that immerses you in the country's untamed landscapes. It's an adventure that lets you test your physical and mental limits while exploring some of Europe's last remaining wilderness places. You bring memories of a land as enchanting as it is wide with you as you travel across uninhabited terrains, take in the abundant wildlife, and take in the breathtaking vistas.

**Adventurous Pursuits: ATV, Snowmobile, Rafting, and More**
Iceland is a sanctuary for adventure seekers with its magnificent scenery and rugged terrain. In this chapter, we shall examine some of the most exciting and heart-pounding activities available to you in this Nordic wonderland. Iceland provides a wide range of daring activities that will leave you with priceless memories, including

exploring rocky terrains on an ATV, tearing across frozen glaciers on a snowmobile, and rafting through thrilling river rapids.

**ATV:** Iceland's Rugged Terrains Explored Taking an All-Terrain Vehicle is one of the greatest ways to experience Iceland's vast and varied landscapes (ATV). ATV tours are available for riders of all skill levels, whether experts or novices. You'll go on exhilarating off-road excursions under the direction of knowledgeable instructors that take you through lava deserts, volcanic fields, and other difficult terrain that is not normally accessible. ATVs' strength and adaptability let you easily navigate over difficult terrain, giving you a close-up view of Iceland's unadulterated beauty.

**Snowmobile:** Thrills in the Glaciers and Frozen Wonderlands Imagine navigating beautiful white glaciers quickly while encircling mountains covered in snow and towering ice formations. In Iceland, snowmobiling is a thrilling activity that lets you discover the icy beauties of this magnificent nation. You'll fly across huge glacier plains, followed by knowledgeable instructors and outfitted with specialist equipment. You'll experience an adrenaline rush as you negotiate slippery turns. Snowmobiling in Iceland will leave you in awe of the country's glacial landscapes, whether you decide to go on a guided trip or set off on your own.

**Rafting:** Taking on the Rapids White water rafting in Iceland is an absolute must-do sport for everyone looking for an exhilarating water adventure. Untamed rivers in the nation offer some of the most thrilling rapids, ensuring an adrenaline rush unlike anything else. You will navigate through strong currents, whirling eddies, and tumbling waterfalls while surrounded by breathtaking natural surroundings and assisted by knowledgeable rafting experts. Everyone can enjoy this heart-pounding thrill thanks to Iceland's many river systems, which provide differing difficulty levels for novice and expert rafters.

**Caving:** Iceland's Underground Wonders: An Exploration A secret world of fascinating caves created by volcanic activity and glacial pressures lies beneath Iceland's breathtaking landscapes. Caving excursions provide a rare chance to explore the depths of these subterranean wonders, including ancient lava tunnels and ice caves. You'll crawl, climb, and squeeze your way through complex cave networks while outfitting with helmets, headlamps, and knowledgeable guides while taking in the breathtaking ice formations, stalactites, and stalagmites. These underground explorations offer a fascinating look at Iceland's geological marvels and a chance to experience nature's craftsmanship up close.

**Glacier Hiking:** Walking on Giants of Ice What better way to see the magnificence of Iceland's magnificent glaciers than by going on a glacier hiking expedition? You'll go on crampons and hike on the icy surfaces of these frozen giants under the guidance of knowledgeable mountaineers. The glaciers' vivid blue tones and the expansive views of the surrounding landscapes will captivate you as you navigate crevasses and explore ice tunnels. A remarkable journey, glacier trekking immerses you in the pristine splendor of Iceland's frozen landscape.

Iceland's adventurous activities provide a starting point for exploration, allowing you to interact in exhilarating and unforgettable ways with the nation's stunning landscapes. Whether you decide to take an ATV tour, race through glaciers on a snowmobile, navigate the rapids while white water rafting, explore secret caverns, or stroll across stunning glaciers, each activity offers an adrenaline rush and the chance to get close to Iceland's unspoiled, natural beauty. So be ready to pack your bags and head to this paradise for adventure seekers to make memories that will last a lifetime.

### Snorkeling and Diving: Discovering Iceland's Underwater World

Under the surface of Iceland's icy seas, a brand-new adventure awaits in its wild, gorgeous surroundings. Iceland's geological fault lines are home to various aquatic life, geothermal vents, and otherworldly clarity underwater, all of which can be explored while snorkeling or scuba diving there. This thrilling journey is a tale of wonder and adventure, a narrative of courageous people who battle the cold to learn the mysteries of the deep.

### The Allure of Silfra

Silfra, the breathtaking freshwater fissure found inside Thingvellir National Park, must be brought up while discussing diving in Iceland. This dive location is well-known for its crystal-clear waters, ensuring visibility that frequently exceeds 100 meters—a trait uncommon in the diving industry. Divers have the incredible opportunity to touch the North American and the Eurasian tectonic plates simultaneously at Silfra, located in the rift between them. Additionally, the water that fills this gap comes from a neighboring glacier and through years of natural filtration in subterranean lava fields, giving it an unmatched purity that is safe to consume even while diving.

### PADI and Dry Suit Diving

Diving and snorkeling in warmer climates necessitate more preparation than diving and snorkeling in Iceland. Dry suits are used instead of standard wet suits to keep body heat in. The Professional

Association of Diving Instructors (PADI) offers dry suit certification training for those who are unfamiliar with them. These courses are crucial for ensuring comfort and safety during dives. Even if they are a little more work, these preparations provide a special and close interaction with the underwater environment of Iceland, making every minute of the extra effort worthwhile.

## Otherworldly Exploration in the North

Even though Silfra frequently grabs the spotlight, diving options in Iceland go far beyond this geological wonder. Consider Strytan, a hydrothermal vent in the northern Icelandic fjord of Eyjafjörur. Strytan is a physical reminder of the nation's volcanic activity because it is the only spot on Earth where divers can descend a warm-water chimney. Many marine life, including vibrant anemones and playful seals, can be found at this dive location, which is teeming with geothermal energy and heated by the Earth's core.

## Submerged Wonders of the South

Southern Iceland also has distinctive underwater features, not to be outdone. The largest lake on the Reykjanes Peninsula, Kleifarvatn, with impressive geological structures and underwater hot springs. The waters of this lake hide enigmatic vistas of dark sand and soaring underwater rocks. The vibrations and bubbles coming from the hot springs can be felt while diving here, giving the impression that you are in another world.

## Into the Abyss at Davidsgja

The most daring divers are invited to explore Iceland's unknown depths at Davidsgja, a sizable fracture in Lake Thingvallavatn. The spine-chilling mood created by this gaping pit that seems to have no bottom and is lined with impressive lava formations cannot be adequately described. Divers are met by an unnervingly beautiful quiet and the sight of ancient lava rocks, a reminder of Iceland's fiery past, as they descend further into the Davidsgja abyss.

## Snorkeling for All Ages

Snorkeling is a more approachable method to see the underwater beauty of Iceland, even though diving there could seem intense. In locations like Silfra, snorkelers of all skill levels may enjoy the exhilaration of swimming between continents while taking in the same clear seas as the divers below. Snorkeling in Iceland's distinctive waterways is an adventure and a way to enjoy the nation's breathtaking natural beauty, regardless of age or degree of experience.

Adventurers, scientists, and nature lovers can explore Iceland's underwater realm as a previously unexplored frontier. The pure transparency of Silfra, the geothermal marvels of Strytan and Kleifarvatn, and the commanding depths of Davidsgja all offer a view into an undersea world that is both breathtakingly beautiful and singular. Iceland's underwater scenery will leave you with life-changing experiences and tales to tell, whether you're an experienced diver or an avid snorkeler. Iceland's icy waters will warm your spirit with a well-planned trip and expose an astonishing underwater world that will astound you.

# Chapter 4: Cities and Culture

**Reykjavík: A Journey into the Creative and Lively Capital**

**The Rich Historical Tapestry of Reykjavík**

Looking into Reykjavk's past will immerse you in a saga that rivals the best of Icelandic literature for gripping news. The city is known as the capital of the most northern country in the world. It was established in 874 AD by Norse explorer Ingólfur Arnarson. It didn't experience significant expansion or development until the 18th century when it was granted town status and a 19th-century modernization boom. Then Reykjavik grew into the thriving capital it is today. The rbr Open Air Museum, a rich emblem of this historical journey, recreates the town's previous appearance and invites visitors to experience life in Iceland in the past.

**Reykjavík: An Energetic Hub of Cultural Activity**

Artistic and intellectual interests are abundant in Reykjavk's cultural landscape. Here, traditional legacy and contemporary ingenuity blend. The largest visual arts museum in Iceland, Reykjavik Art Museum, exemplifies this combination. It houses works by some of the most well-known painters in the nation. It displays an intriguing fusion of modern and contemporary art, guaranteeing an immersive experience for art fans.

## The Iconic Landmarks of Reykjavík

Hallgrmskirkja shines as a beacon among these tales, each of which may be found in Reykjavk's various corners. This majestic church, which bears Hallgrmur Pétursson's name, was built to breathtaking architectural standards. Its distinctive style, influenced by the basalt lava flows of Iceland's terrain, highlights the city's innate connection to its natural surroundings. You are rewarded for climbing to the top of this famous building with an incredible aerial view of the city that perfectly encapsulates the spirit of Reykjavik.

## The Allure of Reykjavík's Streets

The streets of Reykjavik throb with life outside the confines of formalized cultural facilities. Laugavegur, the major thoroughfare for shopping, provides evidence of this vibrancy. It exudes a charm that draws both locals and visitors since it has charming boutiques, cutting-edge fashion stores, and welcoming cafés. The city's vivid and provocative street murals lend yet another element to its creative vibrancy.

## Harpa Concert Hall: A Jewel by the Sea

The Harpa Concert Hall is where Reykjavik's architectural brilliance reaches its pinnacle. This magnificent building, which the Old Harbor tucks away, reflects the vivid vitality of the city through the dynamic play of light and shadow on its geometric glass front. Harpa is an architectural marvel and the location of the Icelandic Symphony Orchestra and the Icelandic Opera.

## When Reykjavík Lights Up

Reykjavk transforms into a hive of nocturnal festivities when the sun sets. The city's nightlife is just as captivating as its daytime attractions. It has vibrant music venues where local bands serenade guests with various genres and throbbing nightclubs that lure audiences with addictive dance beats. Reykjavk has an irresistible charm after dark, whether you're looking to unwind with a drink in a welcoming pub or immerse yourself in the local music scene.

Reykjavk is more than simply a city; it's an experience because of its rich cultural heritage, historical roots, and distinctive attractions. The city embodies an alluring fusion of legacy and modernity, from the echoes of the past at the rbr Museum to the contemporary extravaganza of Harpa Concert Hall, from the artistic manifestations bordering Laugavegur to the exuberant energy that lights up the night. This most northern capital firmly demonstrates that cultural diversity or the ability to inspire and enchant are not related to size.

## Vik and Coastal Wonders: Black Sand Beaches, Caves, and Rock Formations

The intriguing settlement of Vik is located in Iceland, a country of striking contrasts and stunning scenery. Vik, located at the country's southernmost point, is a tribute to nature's majesty and steadfast strength. Every black sand beach, towering cliff, and complicated rock formation exude breathtaking beauty that beckons adventurers and culture seekers to discover its mysteries.

## From Settlement to Scenic Wonderland

Vik's modest roots may be traced to the Viking Age when maritime inhabitants made it a hub for trade and fishing. From these humble beginnings, the hamlet developed as its inhabitants adapted to the harsh environment and created a way of life that complemented the cycles of nature. Despite its small size and remote location, Vik has been able to thrive and forge a rich, unique cultural identity thanks to its advantageous location along the south coast and closeness to productive fishing areas.

## Black Sands and Basalt Columns: Reynisfjara Beach

Reynisfjara Beach must be seen to comprehend Vik's attraction. Reynisfjara is renowned for having some of the strangest-colored sands in the world and is frequently cited as one of the most stunning non-tropical beaches. The sight of the pitch-black space under the frequently grey sky produces a mesmerizing, even bizarre mood.

But Reynisfjara's wonders go beyond its distinctive sands. The unique basalt column structures on the shore are evidence of Iceland's volcanic past. These dark, polygonal columns have an almost carved appearance, creating an organic structure created by lava that has been slowly cooling. These formations continue their captivating show inside the Hálsanefshellir cave, where further mystery lies.

## Reynisdrangar: Sea Stacks of Legend

The Reynisdrangar sea stacks guard Reynisfjara from a short distance offshore. Like so much of Iceland's topography, they were created by volcanic activity and the unrelenting Atlantic waves. The more poetic explanation for their existence, according to Icelandic folklore, is that they were once trolls caught by dawn and turned into stone for all time.

**Dyrhólaey: A Panoramic Vista and Puffin Paradise**

Dyrhólaey, a tiny peninsula or promontory, is located just west of Vik and offers a beautiful view of the nearby coastal beauties. Miles of black beaches, a curving shoreline, and the glaciers of Mrdalsjökull and Eyjafjallajökull may all be seen from its highest elevations.

In addition to offering unmatched views, Dyrhólaey is a sanctuary for animals, especially seabirds. During the summer, it serves as a nesting area for puffins, Iceland's endearing and unofficial avian mascots. Their bright beaks and jovial personalities make for a lovely spectacle when set against the wild grandeur of the surroundings.

**Cultural Attractions: Unveiling Vik's Traditions and Heritage**

While nature provides a wonderful experience, Vik's cultural events and attractions help visitors better appreciate the region's history. The neighborhood church, a small, starkly white structure overlooks the settlement, is located there. Its straightforward, unpretentious beauty supports the community's steadfast faith and fortitude.

The Vikurprjón Wool Workshop provides information about the history of sheep farming in the region and the craft of Icelandic knitting. Visitors can observe local artists at work as they produce traditional woolen products that replicate patterns and methods from ages past.

**Food and Festivities: Delving into the Local Flavor**

A crucial aspect of the Vik experience is trying authentic Icelandic cuisine. Every meal is an opportunity to dig into the country's culinary culture, from the day's fresh fish at neighborhood restaurants to handmade skyr, a type of thick, creamy yogurt particular to Iceland.

Festivals play a significant role in Vik's cultural calendar as well. The Vikurfélag Summer Festival, a vibrant occasion that honors the season with music, dance, and food, is the most notable. It perfectly captures the neighborhood's character, with residents and visitors savoring the long Arctic summer days.

Along with the breathtaking works of nature, the village of Vik is home to a vibrant tapestry of Icelandic culture. It is a location that depicts a village that lives on the border of the Arctic Circle and provides travelers with a distinctive fusion of scenic and cultural delights that stay in their minds long after the trip is over.

## Akureyri: The Gem of the North and Its Tranquil Charms

Akureyri's history began in the ninth century when Norse chieftain Helgi the Lean arrived in Eyjafjörur. Over the years, the town changed from a little fishing community to a prosperous commercial center, especially after establishing a Danish trading station in the 16th century. The 19th century, however, was when Akureyri started to take off. An economic boom by establishing the Kaupfélag Eyfiringa co-operative store in 1882 encouraged a population increase. It cultivated a rich cultural heritage that is still there today.

## Witnessing Faith: The Akureyrarkirkja

The Akureyrarkirkja, perched on a hill in the middle of the city, is a marvel of architecture that perfectly captures the tranquil and ethereal spirit of Akureyri. The church was constructed in 1940 by renowned

Icelandic architect Gujón Samelsson and is recognized for its modernist design and towering stature, serving as a potent religious icon for the neighborhood. Large stained-glass windows in the building depict biblical events, and a ship hanging from the roof represents an ancient Nordic custom of defending mariners. Each step you take up the church stairs mirrors the town's history, and they conclude with a panoramic view of the town and the surrounding fjords and mountains.

## Cultural Legacy: The Nonni House and Beyond

Visits to the Nonni House immerse visitors in Akureyri's thriving literary scene. Jón Sveinsson, also known as Nonni, wrote his well-known children's stories in this modest wooden cottage in the late 19th and early 20th centuries. The museum honors his life and creative output while showcasing the simplicity and tenacity of early Icelandic life.

Akureyri's dedication to culture is evident in its festivals and events. The Akureyri Art Summer is a three-month-long cultural festival transforming the town into a thriving cultural center with art exhibitions, music, theater, and poetry readings. Meanwhile, the Akureyri International Music Festival features national and international artists and presents a wide variety of classical and modern music.

## A Natural Haven: The Akureyri Botanical Garden and Eyjafjörður

The Akureyri Botanical Garden provides a peaceful haven in the middle of the cityscape. This lush refuge, the world's most northerly botanical park, is home to a remarkable array of Arctic and subarctic species, many indigenous to Iceland. Every garden area reveals a different aspect of nature's richness, serving as an outdoor encyclopedia of plants for casual guests and botany specialists.

Akureyri offers the neighboring Eyjafjörur fjord, the longest fjord in Iceland, for people seeking outdoor adventures. Many activities have as their backdrop the amazing beauty of it. Tourists and locals go whale watching or take gorgeous excursions along the rocky shorelines during summer. While the fjord is painted white and blue in the winter, it is transformed into an enchanting environment for skiing, snowboarding, and spotting the elusive northern lights.

**The Heartbeat of Akureyri: Its People and Traditions**

Beyond its stunning scenery and fascinating past, Akureyri is charming due to its kind and outgoing residents. The custom of "rntur," a weekend ritual that involves locals visiting numerous pubs and bars in a welcoming, social gathering, perfectly captures the camaraderie that permeates the area. These customs and the residents' enthusiasm for preserving their town's history contribute to Akureyri's enchantment.

These factors combine to make Akureyri an alluring location. Iceland's wild, resilient, and breathtakingly gorgeous personality is reflected in the city's serene charms, rich historical past, and thriving cultural life.

## Icelandic Culture: Traditions, Folklore, Art, and Music

The sagas, epic tales from the Viking Age that still have meaning for contemporary Icelanders are central to Icelandic culture. These sagas, written in the 13th and 14th centuries, feature vivid characters, tense feuds, and complicated societal interactions. They support their culture and provide a rich window into the lives and ideals of their forefathers. The fact that the sagas are still influential today shows how important they are to shaping Icelandic culture.

## Ásatrú: An Ancient Belief Revived

The spiritual practices of the ancient Norsemen are still alive and well among the beautiful landscapes and powerful volcanoes. The religion known as Satr, a contemporary resurgence of ancestors' doctrines, links Icelanders to their Viking ancestors. This polytheistic religion honors gods like Odin and Thor and reflects virtues like honor, friendliness, and a connection to nature. Therefore, Satr serves as a spiritual link connecting the past and present.

## Elves and Trolls: Tales from the Hidden World

Icelandic culture is profoundly mystical. Folktales about trolls, elves, and hidden folk (or "huldufólk") fascinate residents and tourists. These supernatural beings are frequently portrayed as the land's fellow citizens who are intertwined into the fabric of daily life. Even now, road-building initiatives might be changed to prevent disturbing rocks where elves are said to live.

## Language and Literature: The Heart of Icelandic Identity

The Icelandic language is another foundation of the nation's cultural history, a linguistic gem that has remained mostly unaltered since Old Norse. The country's culture is extremely proud of its literary and linguistic roots. This can be seen in the impressive body of works from acclaimed authors such as Nobel laureate Halldór Laxness, detective novelist Arnaldur Indriðason, and crime fiction writer Yrsa

Sigurðardóttir. Iceland produces more books per person than any other nation due to its entrenched love of literature.

## Icelandic Art: A Canvas of Creativity

Icelandic artistic expression covers a wide range, with influences ranging from conventional Nordic aesthetics to experimental avant-garde movements. This variety in art reflects the variety in Icelandic landscapes, which range from tranquil fjords to rough volcanic terrain. A trip to an Icelandic art gallery or museum reveals a world where traditional themes and modern designs coexist. Artists like Erro, one of Iceland's most well-known contemporary artists, provide perspectives on this varied artistic scene.

## Harmony of Sound: The Icelandic Music Scene

Icelandic culture places a high value on music, which ranges from deep folk melodies to modern pop and rock. With the popularity of bands like Sigur Rós, known for their ethereal sounds, and Of Monsters and Men, recognized for their infectious indie-pop compositions, the nation's music scene has gained international attention. Attendees can see the harmonious fusion of the old and new at festivals and performances held throughout the year, bringing the bustling music scene to life. Icelandic music plays a crucial part in the country's cultural identity because of its exceptional capacity to convey the strength of its landscapes, history, and people.

As demonstrated, Icelandic culture is a fabric rich in tradition, creativity, and history. It displays a strong bond with the land and harmony between holding on to the past and embracing the future. One can learn more about and develop a greater appreciation for

84

Iceland's distinctive cultural legacy by investigating its sagas, spiritual practices, folklore, language, literature, art, and music.

## Icelandic Cuisine: Sampling Traditional Dishes and Local Delicacies

Icelandic food invites you on a historical culinary trip with robust dishes created out of necessity in the country's harsh but abundant climate. Many traditional dinners feature seafood as the star ingredient, with a colorful range of fresh fish sourced from the nearby, chilly North Atlantic waters. Enjoy tender salmon or beautifully cooked fish, two meals representative of the nation's relationship to the sea. Icelandic langoustine, a lobster-like crustacean, is another nautical delicacy best enjoyed with melted butter to highlight its sweet, delicious flavor.

The mainstay of Icelandic meat recipes may be found inland if you focus on the venerable Icelandic lamb. These lambs produce delicate, mildly gamey, and flavorful meat while grazing on lush pastures and being nourished by clean, unpolluted air. Try this well-known ingredient in kjötspa, a classic beef soup bursting with chunky root vegetables and flavorful herbs. This meal perfectly captures the coziness and coziness of home cooking.

### Indulge in Unique Icelandic Delicacies

Iceland has mouthwatering regional specialties that challenge and entice you if you're an adventurous eater. The most notorious of these is hákarl, fermented shark meat with a flavor and perfume as unique as its preparation. This unusual meal, with its potent, ammonia-rich flavor, is a monument to the ingenuity and tenacity of the Icelandic people, a means of surviving the harsh Nordic winters.

On the meatier side is svi, a singed sheep's head that is a nod to the country's past when no scrap was thrown away. This dish invites guests to participate in a custom that dates back to the Viking Age, making it both a cultural and culinary experience.

**Sweet Endings and Icelandic Libations**

Also suited to people with a sweet craving is Icelandic cuisine. Enjoy a mouthful of skyr, a dairy item between yogurt and cheese, or a kleinur, twisted doughnuts delicately powdered with sugar. Any Icelandic meal ends with skyr, which can be eaten plain or spiced with a drizzle of honey or a handful of fresh berries. It is a cooling and nourishing dessert.

Of course, visiting Iceland for food and drink wouldn't be complete without trying local specialties. Hákarl is typically served with brennivn, a strong schnapps popularly known as "Black Death." If you'd like something less powerful, you might be interested in Iceland's growing craft beer culture. Taste the purity and soul of the nation itself as you sip drinks made with ingredients like Icelandic barley and glacial water and inspired by the breathtaking environment.

**Icelandic Cuisine: A Feast of Culture and Heritage**

Every region of Iceland provides culinary experiences rich in cultural value, from bustling urban centers to calm coastal and rural settings. Icelandic food offers a deeper understanding of the nation's heritage and interaction with its natural surroundings, in addition to satisfying the body and the soul. Every food and drink in Iceland is an opportunity to discover and connect with this magical place, whether trying local specialties, experiencing **traditional** cuisine, or simply relishing a home-brewed craft beer.

# Chapter 5: Best Places to Stay in Iceland

Iceland, a country of snow-capped mountains and cold fjords, is home to beautiful places that entice travelers worldwide. Accommodation options on this North Atlantic island are as magnificent and varied as its landscapes. Pack your luggage and prepare for an Icelandic adventure, and use our guide to help you decide where to lay your head down after a long day.

## Reykjavík and Surroundings

Reykjavk, the capital of Iceland, combines global flare with the coziness of a tiny town. There are numerous places to stay here. The Alda Hotel offers expansive city views and the surrounding mountain range. In contrast, the 101 Hotel, located in the city's art area, combines a sleek, minimalist style with welcoming comfort. The Reykjavk Residence Hotel provides apartment-style lodging with fully functional kitchens for people seeking cozy comfort. These city treasures cost between $150 and $350 a night to stay at.

## Farm Stays: Experiencing Authentic Icelandic Farm Life

You may fully immerse yourself in a pastoral haven by choosing a farm vacation. Visitors can experience a piece of traditional Icelandic life at these rural retreats. Visit Ytri Vk, a working farm that doubles as a hotel, in the middle of the country. Enjoy freshly prepared meals and roaming animals while enjoying the breathtaking seaside views. Such accommodations often range in price from $90 to $200 per night.

## Coastal Village Accommodations

Iceland's coastline communities provide quiet, scenic lodgings for those who are at heart mariners. Choose a room with a view at the Fosshotel in Hellnar, a small town on the Snfellsnes Peninsula, or travel to Husavik, the center of whale-watching, and stay at the Cape Hotel, which offers plenty of harbor views. These boating getaways cost between $120 and $280.

## Mountain Huts and Lodges

Mountaineers and solitary people, be ready to be mesmerized. Iceland's secluded mountain huts and resorts, like Kerlingarfjöll Mountain Resort, make for dreamy retreats. In these cabins buried away in the rocky hills, drift off under a blanket of stars or even the elusive Northern Lights. You should budget between $80 and $160 for such peaceful seclusion.

## Accommodations near Major Attractions

Staying close to some of Iceland's top sights, including the Golden Circle, the Jökulsárlón glacial lagoon, or the fabled Skógafoss waterfall, has its appeal. Consider staying at the Hotel Geysir, which provides proximity to the famous lagoon and direct views of the geyser, or the stylish Fosshotel Glacier Lagoon. These picture-perfect lodgings cost between $150 and $300 per night.

## Camping and Glamping Options

Take advantage of Iceland's numerous camping and glamping alternatives to embrace the call of the wild. Nothing quite compares to the pleasure of camping beneath Iceland's otherworldly skies, whether you want to set up your tent in the verdant órsmörk valley or choose a luxurious bell tent at the Buubble, "5 million stars" hotel. While glamping can cost up to $200 per night, camping costs between $10 and $20 per person.

## Vacation Rentals and Holiday Homes

Several vacation rentals and holiday homes are available for people who value independence and privacy. Anyone looking for a home away from home can find one in a rural Selfoss house or a contemporary flat in Akureyri. Budget-friendly lodging costs $80 a night and ranges to $300 or more for luxurious hotels.

## Hotels and Hostels

Hotels and hostels cater to a variety of travel types and budgets. There are accommodations for every taste, from chic hotels like the Canopy by Hilton in the center of Reykjavik to budget-friendly hostels like the quirky, vibrant Kex Hostel. Hostels can start as little as $20 for a dorm bed, while hotel rates range from $150 to $350.

The place you stay in Iceland ultimately serves as more than just a place to sleep. It's a crucial component of your journey and a continuation of your adventure in this enchanted place. So you can be sure to make lifelong memories whether you stay in a posh metropolitan hotel or a modest mountain cabin.

# Chapter 6: Practical Tips and Useful Information

Travelers worldwide are constantly drawn to Iceland by its ethereal beauty, breathtaking scenery, and dynamic culture. It is crucial to be organized and knowledgeable when you plan your trip to this region of fire and ice. This article clarifies key travel considerations for Iceland, including budgeting, budgeting options, safety precautions, and sustainability rules.

## Transportation: Car Rentals, Public Transport, and Getting Around

Although the idea of a trip to Iceland conjures up thoughts of breathtaking natural beauty, practical issues like transportation take precedence. Your travels will go more smoothly and enjoyably if you have reliable, affordable transportation.

A car rental may be the best option for travelers who want to experience Iceland's length and breadth at their speed while riding in their little bubble. Various automobiles are available from companies like "Blue Car Rental" and "Cars Iceland" to meet different demands. Ensure you are familiar with Iceland's driving laws because they vary greatly from those in other nations.

However, Iceland's public transportation system provides a dependable substitute if you'd prefer to give up the driving seat. Buses like Strtó provide a wide network of services throughout the nation. Additionally, enjoyable maritime routes to islands that wouldn't otherwise be reachable are made possible by ferries like "Eimskip" and "Seatours."

## Budget and Expenses: Tips for Managing Your Budget and Finding Deals

Although an unusual place, Iceland is frequently thought of as being expensive. However, visiting Iceland need not be expensive if you take a thoughtful approach and exercise some caution.

First, think about going when it's not as busy. Even though Iceland is less crowded and more affordable than during the summer, its fascination does not fade. While traveling, eating local cuisine can add flavor and ease the strain on your wallet. Local specialties are available at places like "Icelandic Street Food" in Reykjavik that are reasonably priced.

Utilize technology to locate the greatest offers. Platforms for lodging and tour booking, such as "Booking.com" and "Guide to Iceland," frequently provide discounted rates and packaged deals. Keep a look out for free attractions, such as the Aurora Borealis in the winter or geothermal springs like "Nauthólsvk" near Reykjavik.

## Safety and Health: Recommendations for a Safe and Enjoyable Trip

Never put off thinking about your health and safety while traveling. This is true of Iceland as well. The nation frequently has unpredictably bad weather, which makes outdoor activities potentially difficult.

Travel insurance is not an area where you should skimp. Make sure you have coverage for emergencies and unforeseen circumstances. Understanding Iceland's topography and weather patterns is essential for hikers and adventurers. Real-time weather and traffic conditions updates can be found on websites like "Safe Travel Iceland."

Vigilance is essential, even in cities. Although Iceland has a low crime rate, protecting your possessions and personal information is always wise.

## Sustainability and Environmental Considerations: Guidelines for Responsible Travel

Being an environmentally conscientious tourist is more vital than ever in today's age. It is a gift to see Iceland's untamed, natural beauty, and it is up to us to leave as little of an impression as possible.

An excellent place to start is by adhering to the official recommendations provided by the Icelandic Environment Agency. Visitors are urged to stay on designated pathways, avoid littering, and desist from harming wildlife. Using eco-friendly tour operators and green lodgings can decrease your carbon footprint.

Consider the long-term effects of your activities as well. Even though they may appear harmless initially, activities that degrade local ecosystems or souvenirs created from endangered species can have disastrous long-term repercussions.

Remember that the trip to Iceland is an opportunity to appreciate and conserve the planet's beauty for future generations, not merely to satisfy our wanderlust. Be knowledgeable and sensitive to the world we share to make your trip to this amazing country unforgettable and responsible.

# Conclusions

It is important to reflect on and savor our amazing adventure as the night sky paints a poetic silhouette of the dancing auroras on the final page of the "Iceland Travel Guide." This travelogue has been more than just a map to take us through Iceland's breathtaking landscapes. Iceland has sprung from its destruction like a phoenix, symbolizing the human spirit's unwavering will to live. It has revealed Iceland's magnificence in its unadulterated, natural state—a region of fire and ice that carries the wounds of nature's wrath and the allure of her kindness.

We started by sketching the incredible scenery of Iceland, including its freezing glaciers, scalding geysers, thundering waterfalls, volcanic mountains, and black sand beaches. We traveled through Reykjavik's vibrant city, got lost in the maze of Icelandic legend, tasted the local cuisine, and were in awe of the people's fortitude and hospitality. We understood the power of sustainability, the reverence for nature's energies, and the allure of stillness.

Our journey was more than simply a demonstration of the sensory delights a spotless setting can provide. The intricacies of a civilization shaped by seclusion and the powerful powers of the Earth were intimately encountered. It was both a rapid trip into the future and a dive into the depths of history. We have all worked to make this book a moving window into Iceland's soul and a catalyst for a more in-depth understanding of this extraordinary nation.

We are reminded of the wealth of memories we bring back as we pack our luggage and go on this virtual journey. Knowing that these experiences have permanently changed how we view travel and nature, our emotions are heavy with happiness and expectation. The guide offered tips and resources to help you preserve your experiences in honor of these memories, from keeping a travel journal to setting up online archives. These memories serve as more than just examples of the past; they also serve as a source of happiness, motivation, and wisdom for the future.

There are a ton of other breathtaking vistas in the world that lies beyond the rocky cliffs of Iceland. This guide's concluding chapters inspired your yearning for equally alluring locales like Norway's fjords, Canada's Rockies, or New Zealand's alpine landscapes. Each one is an invitation to venture beyond the familiar, appreciate our planet's true beauty, and keep discovering the countless beauties that are still to be discovered.

This book fulfilled its promise to provide a thorough, engaging, and instructive tour of Iceland by capturing readers' imaginations and creating vivid mental images. It served as your dependable travel companion, assisting you as you navigate the wilderness and the wonders of Iceland, providing you with priceless knowledge and sound counsel, spinning tales, and helping you come to understand this stunning setting and its kind inhabitants.

This journey was not just about the places we visited but also about the memories it left behind. The realization that travel involves more than just moving from one location to another would be the most important lesson to learn from this book. The internal alteration takes place in response to the scope of nature, the diversity of cultures, and the strength of the community. It is the process of discovering oneself while viewing the world in which we live.

I hope this book will lead you into the heart of Iceland. Remember J.R.R. Tolkien's wise words, "Not all people who travel are lost," as this voyage comes to a close. Let us commit to this great voyage of exploration and discovery, using the world as our playground and curiosity as our compass.

Made in United States
Troutdale, OR
11/16/2023

14264847R20056